❝ Teachers who are trying to really listen to and learn from their students in math class will find a lot of helpful guidance here. Gina Picha stays true to her belief in children as powerful mathematical sense-makers while explicitly addressing ways to help them develop mathematical identity and autonomy in empowering ways. ❞

Ruth Parker, mathematics educator, author and co-developer of *Number Talks*

❝ Finally, we have a guidebook for the most crucial teaching moment of our math block! By conferring we teach so the learning endures for life. The strategies Gina Picha presents will transform our mathematics classrooms and communities, teach us to know students' strengths and learning goals through our strategic listening and questioning, and simplify our instruction through authentic conversation, all while empowering our students with confidence in their identity as mathematicians. *Conferring in the Math Classroom* is a must-have resource for every math teacher. ❞

Corinna Green, Elementary Instructional Coach & Teaching Consultant

❝ Packed full of examples, illustrations, and charts, this book truly provides strong support for learning to talk with small groups of students to support and extend their mathematical thinking. At the heart of Gina's book is developing positive math identities with students (and teachers). Beautifully written and immensely useful. ❞

Jennifer Bay-Williams, professor, University of Louisville

❝ Engaging in conversations with students about their mathematical thinking gives teachers a lens into how their students are currently thinking about the key ideas being addressed in a lesson. In *Conferring in the Math Classroom*, Gina Picha masterfully outlines how teachers can plan for and facilitate meaningful math conferences with their students. The book is full of examples and resources to make this routine easy to implement. If you are a teacher, math coach, or other educational leader looking to elevate students' mathematical discourse, then this book is for you. ❞

Mike Flynn, author of *Beyond Answers*

❝ The ability to confer well is the teacher magic that meets children right where they are to give them perfectly dosed instruction. So many of us can do this well in reading and writing and now we finally have a guide to help us create these powerful math conversations and invitations as well. Let the math magic begin! ❞

Jen McDonough, coauthor of *Conferring with Young Writers: What to Do When You Don't Know What to Do*

❝ Gina writes, 'To have a positive math identity, a person needs to believe that they are a mathematician.' In literacy, we often refer to our students as readers and writers, but do we do the same when it comes to math? *Conferring in the Math Classroom* not only gives practical advice and tools for growing students in their math understanding, but it also highlights the importance of conferring to build those positive math identities in an environment where students feel safe to take risks. Gina encourages us to draw from student strengths when nudging them forward, and she just might help you reshape your own math identity as well! ❞

Casey Koester, 3rd-grade teacher, M.Ed

❝ I am always in search of professional books that put the mathematics, pedagogy, and implementation support alongside the development of a collaborative classroom community. Gina has gifted us such a book. Each chapter includes thoughtful, practical structures that can be used to elicit and center students' ideas. The focus on listening and observing as students share ideas, elevates the importance of teachers building on students' thinking and strengths to take them further and deeper into the mathematics. The in-practice classroom stories and student examples bring to life a vision of what it looks like to utilize conferring as a daily classroom practice. ❞

Kristin Gray, math educator

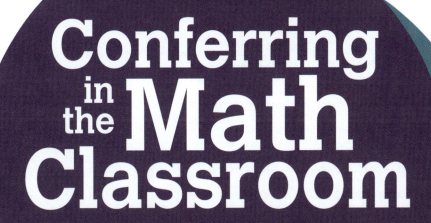

Conferring in the Math Classroom

A Practical Guidebook to Using **5-Minute Conferences** to Grow Confident Mathematicians
K-5

Gina Picha

Foreword by Brian Bushart

www.stenhouse.com

Portsmouth, New Hampshire

www.stenhouse.com

Copyright © 2022 by Gina Picha

All rights reserved. Except for pages in the appendix, which can be photocopied for classroom use, no part of this publication may be reproduced or transmitted in any form or by any means, electronic or mechanical, including photocopy, or any information storage and retrieval system, without permission from the publisher.

Every effort has been made to contact copyright holders and students for permission to reproduce borrowed material. We regret any oversights that may have occurred and will be pleased to rectify them in subsequent reprints of the work.

Table 5.1 adapted from *Principles to Actions: Ensuring Mathematical Success for All*. © 2014 National Council of Teachers of Mathematics. Used by permission of NCTM.

Figures 6.7–6.10: reproduced with permission of The Math Learning Center (mathlearningcenter.org).

Cataloging-in-Publication Data is on file with the Library of Congress.

Cover design, interior design, and typesetting by Page2, LLC, Wayne, NJ.

Printed in the United States of America

This book is printed on paper certified by third-party standards for sustainably managed forestry.

28 27 26 25 24 23 22   4371   9 8 7 6 5 4 3 2 1

To Deric, Nolan, and Cort,
who have always been my inspiration

Contents

Foreword ix

Acknowledgments xi

Preface xii

Part 1 **Math Conferences: What Are They?** 1

    Chapter 1: Defining Math Conferences 3

    Chapter 2: The Similarities and Differences between Math and Literacy Conferences 13

    Chapter 3: Types of Math Conferences 23

Part 2 **Effective Questioning: What Types of Questions Elicit Students' Thinking?** 39

    Chapter 4: Questioning to Promote Thinking and Understanding 41

    Chapter 5: Selecting Questions for Specific Purposes 49

Part 3 **Asset-Based Conferring: How Does Focusing on Students' Strengths Support Them in Making Conjectures?** 61

    Chapter 6: Conferring from Students' Strengths 63

    Chapter 7: Nudging Student Thinking and Inviting Conjecture in *Beyond the Task* Conferences 81

Part 4 **Planning for Success: What Should You Consider before Conferring?** 97

    Chapter 8: Building a Math Community that Fosters Positive Math Identities 99

    Chapter 9: Planning for Data Collection and Analysis 105

    Chapter 10: Planning for the Tricky Parts 117

Appendix A: If-Then Charts 125

Appendix B: Conferring Scenarios 129

Appendix C: Conferring Notes Template 135

References 139

Index 141

Foreword

I've had several epiphanies in my career that have shaped the course of my teaching and my beliefs about how we should best spend our time with students. One of those epiphanies occurred while I was teaching fourth grade in 2008. That year I piloted a math assessment which included interviewing individual students as they solved a problem about four pockets with three coins in each pocket. To be honest, this felt like a tedious and time-consuming way to determine whether my students could multiply four and three, but I couldn't have been more wrong! As I interviewed each student, I was continually amazed at how every single one of them brought something different to the table, whether it was the tool they chose, the way they made sense of the situation, or how they interacted with the numbers. I interviewed twenty-two students and got twenty-two different ways of thinking that all led to the same answer of twelve coins. In that moment it struck me just how vital it is to talk to students and listen to their mathematical ideas. If we're only looking at answers on the page, we're only scratching the surface of what our students understand.

Unfortunately, this epiphany didn't arrive with a handy set of directions or a guidebook about how to make listening to students' thinking a regular, meaningful part of my practice. This is why I'm so excited and thankful for the book you're holding in your hands right now. In *Conferring in the Math Classroom*, Gina has taken years of conferring experience and distilled it down into a coherent and predictable structure for us to follow. She includes thoughtful advice and guidance to help you feel confident about getting started with having short, frequent conversations with your students about their mathematical ideas. And let me tell you, once you get started, you'll be hooked!

Are you brand new to conferring? Do you already confer with students during reading and writing, but you're not quite sure what that might look like during math? Are you coaching teachers around conferring in math class? This book is for all of you! Gina thoughtfully breaks down the components of a five-minute math conference into manageable parts. They're easy to remember and with a little practice, you'll feel comfortable using this structure. It'll be even more beneficial if you can read this book with a colleague or two. Once you get started, you'll become fascinated with your students' thinking, and you'll feel like you're going to burst if you can't share and talk about it with someone else. And that will be just the beginning of your conferring journey. This is a book that rewards revisiting. As soon as you get some conferring experience under your belt, you'll be able to come back to this book and deepen your expertise with choosing which questions to ask, identifying students' strengths, and nudging your students to think more deeply about the mathematics they're learning.

Conferring in the Math Classroom is ready to support you every step of the way. Gina's extensive experience as an instructional coach shines through every chapter. Gina knows that we're often excited when we try something new, but we can also get overwhelmed and worry that we might be doing it wrong. She advises us to give ourselves permission to not know everything. Go into conferences curious about what your students are thinking, rather than worrying about whether you have all the right answers. There are a lot of decisions to make, but as Gina wisely points out, there are so many *right* decisions to make. Like a good coach, Gina reassures us that with practice we'll eventually find ourselves in familiar territory. I value the wisdom in her words, "If you get off track, don't panic. Stop and think about what you really want to know and try again" (p. 59).

While listening to student thinking is fascinating—and you won't want to stop once you get started—it's important to remember this isn't just for our benefit. It's vitally important for our students too. Listening to student thinking helps us build positive relationships with each one of our students. Our students are watching us. They observe how we interact with them (*if* we interact with them) and they observe the words we say (as well as the words we don't say). Gina's conferring guidebook provides an easy-to-follow structure for five-minute conferences that ensures students are learning that their thinking is regularly heard and valued, learning what strengths they have as mathematicians, and being encouraged to deeply explore and share their ideas with the rest of their community. To quote Gina, "Although instructional time is always scarce, developing our students' mathematical thinking will always be time well spent" (p. 47).

So what are you waiting for? It's time to dig into this book! Before you know it, you'll be full of curiosity, pulling up alongside a small group of students, and I can't wait for you to be amazed at what they'll teach you.

– **Brian Bushart**

Acknowledgments

When I think about my passion and love for education, I have always believed it started with Miss Barrett, my fifth-grade teacher. I have never been able to find her, but I hope someday I can tell her what a positive impact she has had on my life. As her student, I started the school year as a little girl that didn't want to go to school and quickly transformed into someone that went to bed each Sunday wishing it was Monday morning. It was because of her that I decided to be a teacher, and I tried each and every day to be as kind, attentive, and patient with my students as she was with us. Thank you, Miss Barrett, for showing me firsthand that we learn the most when we feel a sense of connection and belonging. The importance of developing relationships with my students and creating a safe and welcoming learning environment is the most impactful lesson that I have learned about teaching.

I would also like to thank my editor, Kassia Wedekind, who is not only an incredibly knowledgeable mathematics educator but also the type of writing teacher I wish every student could have. Her feedback left me feeling proud of my work yet eager to make important revisions that would support my readers. The suggestions and nudges that Kassia gave me throughout the writing process are treasured lessons that I will most certainly take with me on my journey as a writer.

In addition to Kassia, I would like to express my gratitude to Susan Benner, Stephanie Levy, Shannon St. Peter, and the entire Stenhouse team. Thank you for making this book come to life in ways that I couldn't even imagine. I'll never be able to find the words to convey just how honored I am to call myself a Stenhouse writer.

I also want to thank all the teachers I have worked alongside throughout the years. I have such fond memories of my days at Joe Lee Johnson Elementary, where I was lucky enough to learn from teachers like Ashley Hentges, Trakasha Paul, and Michael Armstrong. I also want to thank my instructional coaching colleague, Corinna Green. I will always cherish our days as instructional coaches. Thank you for being a source of support and encouragement and helping me to become a better writing teacher! And I want to give a special acknowledgment to my friend and colleague, Brian Bushart. I am extremely lucky to have had the opportunity to learn from you as a teacher, coach, and member of the curriculum team. Your passion for mathematics education and your commitment to doing what's best for every student is admirable and contagious.

I would also like to share my overwhelming gratitude to writers and education experts Lucy Calkins, Carl Anderson, Ralph Fletcher, Cathy Fosnot, Kathy Richardson, Tracy Zager, Dr. Jo Boaler, Sherry Parrish, Ruth Parker, Cathy Humphreys, and so many more. Throughout my teaching career, your books were my mentors and, as anyone who knows me will confirm, my treasured possessions. To this day, your books never stay on my shelves for long. The covers are faded, torn, and bent. The pages are folded over and filled with sticky notes that contain scribblings of my thoughts and ideas. Thank you for the support, knowledge, and endless inspiration.

And my biggest thank you is to Deric, Nolan, and Cort. Thank you for always reminding me that I can do hard things. Without you, this book would have only existed in my dreams. Love you, always.

Preface

As a child, going to Grandma Yario's house for the weekend was one of my favorite things to do. We always had a similar routine. We would go to Elmhurst restaurant, I would order fish sticks, and Grandma would order French onion soup. Next, we would go to the video store to rent a movie. Grandma would always let me pick out any movie, no matter how silly. Then we would stop for ice cream and bring it back to her house and eat it while watching the movie.

Around the time I entered third grade, something else was added to our weekends—math. Grandma had heard that I was having a hard time in math, mostly with telling time and division with remainders. To support me, she bought me countless math workbooks, and we'd do them together. I will always remember this time in my childhood because I felt like Grandma truly believed that I could do well in math. When I was working on math problems or telling time with her, I never felt rushed or anxious. Her patience and constant reassurance that I could do it allowed me to focus on the math rather than my fear of being bad at math.

As the years went by, I began to see myself as someone that could do well in math. I realized that I am capable of working through challenging math problems, and that I actually like the challenge. My journey with mathematics has helped me to realize that, before we can expect children to tell time or figure out what to do with a remainder, we need to teach them to believe that they are already capable of doing mathematics, even when it is hard! This is the lesson that my grandma taught me. It is a lesson that I have carried with me into my teaching career. If we want students to grow as mathematicians, we have to do everything we can to help them develop positive math identities. And I believe the best way to do that is by treating them like mathematicians from the moment they enter our classrooms.

What Is a Math Identity?

Sometimes the phrase *math identity* can be confused with whether or not a person enjoys doing math. This is surely a component of it, but our math identities are affected by more than just our interest in the subject. It starts with our beliefs about what math is and what it isn't. Believing that math is a series of disconnected steps to follow and memorize can negatively affect a person's math identity. Viewing mathematics as purely procedural distorts the subject into something it isn't—a subject most people wouldn't find interesting.

Math identities are shaped by a person's beliefs about their math abilities. If a person believes that some people are more capable of mathematical thinking than others, there is little hope that they will have a positive relationship with mathematics. This mindset is harmful even for those that experience academic success. Positive math identities developed on a foundation of high test scores will crumble at the first sign of failure. Those with truly positive math identities understand that failure is an opportunity to learn and grow. Success in mathematics is not defined by letter grades or our speed in answering math problems. Success in math has more to do with our desire to persevere and get creative when faced with really interesting and challenging problems.

To have a positive math identity, a person needs to believe that they are a mathematician. Being a mathematician means doing math! It also means sharing and learning within a math community. A sense of belonging to some type of math community, whether it be on Twitter, with our families, or with fellow math teachers, supports healthy and positive math identities. It is very difficult to have a positive math identity without doing math!

Teacher Math Identity

Being a math teacher really ups the ante on the importance of positive math identities. Researchers have found that a teacher's beliefs about mathematics can affect their students' beliefs about their abilities to learn math and their math achievement (Beilock, Gunderson, Ramirez, & Levine 2010; Ramirez, Hooper, Kersting, Ferguson, & Yeager 2018). After considering the research, I reflected on my own experiences as a teacher. I remembered a little girl in my class who told her mom that she only wanted to wear dresses to school because that is what I always wore. I'll also never forget a little boy named Jack, who told his mom that she needed to start cutting his apples the way I had during a science lesson. Our students soak in so much more than we might ever know! It makes sense that students are affected by their teachers' relationship with mathematics.

Teachers' math identities are also shaped by their beliefs about their students' abilities to learn mathematics and their abilities to teach mathematics. These additional factors are critically important, because it is possible to have a positive math identity and a negative teacher math identity. As teachers, it is important that we truly believe that all students are capable of the highest levels of mathematics. Simply believing that we are capable mathematicians isn't enough. We must also believe that we are capable of teaching mathematics.

Teacher Math Identity and Conferring

So what does math identity have to do with conferring? Everything! The choice to confer or not to confer can be the difference between creating a traditional math classroom, in which the focus is on teaching specific math skills, or a collaborative math community, in which the focus is on developing a shared understanding of mathematics and growing lifelong mathematicians. Conferring gives students the daily feedback they need to develop confidence in their mathematical abilities and the encouragement they need to engage in collaborative problem solving with their peers. These short five-minute conferences, when done regularly, create the framework for a classroom math community bustling with excited, independent, and confident mathematicians. So let's get started!

Part 1

Math Conferences:

What Are They?

Chapter 1

Defining Math Conferences

> ❝ Chelsea, I noticed you joined five cubes and then seven more. Jaylon, I noticed you put seven cubes together and then joined five more. You both counted twelve in total. Do you think that always happens? Do you think you can join cubes in any order and get the same total? ❞

I love asking young mathematicians questions like these and listening to them reason and grapple with big ideas. In this particular instance, the two first graders disagreed.

Jaylon quickly shared, "You can always do it in any order."

Chelsea looked at me but didn't say anything. "What do you think?" I nudged.

"I don't think it always works. Maybe sometimes," Chelsea whispered.

Conversations like this are powerful tools for mathematics teachers because they give us insight into our students' mathematical thinking and their evolving math identities. Are you wondering why Chelsea whispered? Are you wondering if she always seems cautious when sharing her thinking? Are you curious as to how Jaylon might explain his thinking? I was too, and I planned to do a lot more listening during this conference!

What Exactly Is a Math Conference?

Math conferences are brief conversations that help us understand our students' thinking and provide opportunities to observe our students as they engage in mathematics. These conversations yield important information about the types of mathematical connections and generalizations our students are making as well as how they feel about themselves and their abilities as mathematicians.

While there are different types of math conferences that we will discuss throughout the book, all math conferences include three essential elements: (1) listening and observing, (2) naming students' strengths, and (3) encouraging students to share ideas.

Listening and Observing

Listening and observing are the heart of conferring. Without sitting beside Chelsea and Jaylon, listening to their thinking and paying careful attention to their reactions and expressions, I might have missed Chelsea's hesitant whisper. I might not have caught Jaylon's raised eyebrow when Chelsea replied that joining the cubes in a different order might not always work. Was he rethinking? Did he want to say something more? These observations are so important, and yet without sitting beside students and listening carefully, they are important pieces of information that I might otherwise miss. Furthermore, listening is an important part of fostering students' math identities. When we listen attentively to our students' ideas, we communicate that we are interested in their work, believe in their abilities to reason and make mathematical decisions, and see them as valued members of the math community.

Naming Students' Strengths

When we approach students with the goal of listening intently to their ideas, we are likely to notice the important decisions they make as mathematicians. As I was listening to Jaylon and Chelsea, I paid careful attention to how they were counting, joining, and keeping track of the cubes. I made a mental note of these strengths because I planned to select one strength and name that for Chelsea and Jaylon. This teacher move provides an opportunity to make students' mathematical decisions explicit and transparent for them—and anyone sitting nearby! Since mathematicians often work collaboratively in the classroom, naming strengths is a great way to publicly assign competence to students and to encourage them to view themselves and their peers as capable mathematicians.

Encouraging Students to Share Their Ideas

Another important part of a math conference is encouraging students to share their ideas with their fellow mathematicians in the class. Sometimes teachers invite students to share a strategy or new idea with the classroom math community. Other times students are nudged to share with a partner or small group of students. The purpose of this part of a math conference is to give students frequent opportunities to engage with the math community by sharing their strategies, presenting and defending their ideas, and even challenging the ideas of their peers. Let's take a look at the following math conference with three fifth-grade students to practice identifying these three essential elements of a math conference.

Conferring with Fifth-Grade Mathematicians

One morning I stepped into a fifth-grade classroom where kids were working on adding decimals from a word problem displayed on the classroom projector. Three fifth-grade students, Darlene, Damian, and Chloe, were all working at the same table. Darlene and Damian had base-ten blocks and they were busily representing the decimals .62 and 1.83 and joining them together. I noticed that Chloe was not using the base-ten blocks and was writing something in her notebook.

Darlene and Damian announced, "We got 2.45. That's close to our estimate of 2.60."

Chloe responded, "That's what I got too." I knelt down beside Chloe and couldn't quite make out what she had written in her notebook.

I asked, "Can you tell me about your thinking?" My curiosity seemed to spark Darlene and Damian's interest because they leaned in to take a closer look at Chloe's notebook.

"Well," Chloe said, "I don't really like working with numbers like these. So, I made them into numbers that I like."

I smiled and said, "I do the same thing. As a mathematician, I prefer friendly numbers. Can you tell me what you did?" At this point, Chloe seemed more relaxed and appeared proud to share her work with the growing audience.

She continued, "Well I didn't like .62, so I changed it to .50 and .12. I also didn't like 1.83. So, I changed it to 1.0, .50, and .33" (**Figure 1.1**).

As I listened to Chloe, I really wanted to be sure that I understood her thinking. "So, are you saying that the numbers .50 and .12 are easier to work with than the number .62?"

"Well, yeah," Chloe replied. "Because if I can take out the .50 from both .62 and .83, then I can add .50 and .50 together to make 1."

I wanted to be sure to name this strategy, not only for Chloe but for Darlene and Damian who were listening intently to Chloe's explanation. "So, you decomposed the decimals to make friendly numbers like .50. Then you rearranged the addends so that you could associate the ones that made sense to group together. This is powerful work, Chloe! As a mathematician, you made the important decision to decompose the numbers in a way that made sense to you. I wonder if you could share this thinking with the class during our share out today. I think others would want to try something like this!"

As Chloe beamed, Damian interjected, "I think we kind of did something similar with our base-ten blocks."

FIGURE 1.1

Chloe records her thinking about adding decimals in her notebook

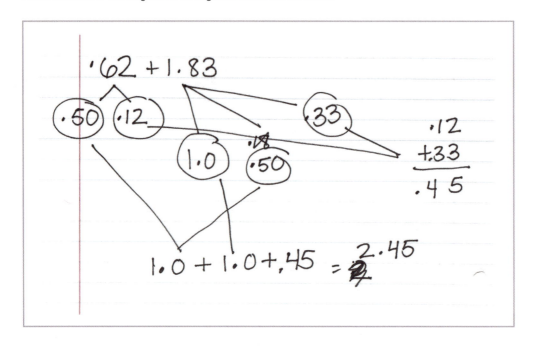

FIGURE 1.2

Damian and Darlene model their thinking for adding 1.83 and .62 with base-ten blocks

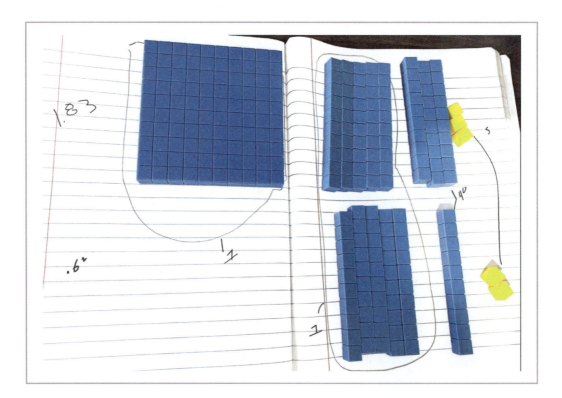

Part 1 Math Conferences: What Are They?

I quickly took advantage of Damian's connection and said, "I think it would be really powerful for your fellow mathematicians to see this problem represented symbolically like Chloe has done as well as visually with base-ten blocks like you did. Do you think you could prepare something to show our math community?" (**See Figure 1.2.**)

This short conference, which lasted about five minutes, focused on uncovering students' thinking and encouraging students to work and share as mathematicians. Just as in all conferences, I started by listening and observing. I asked questions to understand Chloe's work and listened carefully as she and Damian shared their thinking. I decided to explicitly name Chloe's choice to decompose the decimals into friendly numbers. In doing so I validated her ability to make decisions that help her make sense of the mathematics. Finally, I invited all three fifth graders to share their important work, which provided them with further opportunities to engage in deep mathematical thinking and reminded them of their roles as members of a math community.

Two Other Types of Math Conversation

Conferring conversations like the one with Chloe, Damian, and Darlene are intentional and have specific goals—they're my favorite type of mathematical conversation to have with students. But that doesn't mean conferring is the only type of conversation with instructional value. Before we take a deeper look at conferring, let's distinguish it from two other types of conversations: conversations for assessment and conversations to scaffold learning.

TABLE 1.1

Types of Conversations in Mathematics Classrooms

	Description	Purpose	Example	Frequency
Conversations for Assessment	The teacher keeps a record of students' understanding of specific mathematics skills.	To keep a record of students' learning progressions and mastery of skills.	The teacher wants to assess which students have developed an understanding of cardinality and which students are still developing an understanding of this counting principle. In order to learn more, the teacher observes and talks with students. The teacher also keeps an ongoing record to help plan future learning experiences.	Ongoing through observation and interviews.
Conversations to Scaffold Learning	The teacher adjusts the level of rigor by asking students specific questions, prompting specific student actions, or providing students with another resource or tool.	To increase or decrease the level of rigor of an activity to meet the child's needs. The goal is for all children to work within their zones of proximal development.	The teacher notices that a student is successful with measuring a piece of yarn with large paper clips. To challenge the child, the teacher asks if they might like to try it with smaller paper clips. This change in tool will provide an opportunity for the child to compare results of measuring with a smaller unit.	As needed based on teacher observation of student understanding.
Conferences	The teacher elicits student thinking, reinforces specific practices, and nudges students to make generalizations and share their thinking as part of a math community.	To guide students to develop and share their mathematical ideas and to develop healthy identities as valuable members of a community of mathematicians.	The teacher notices that a student is touching each object as they count. The teacher asks the child about their decision to touch each object. Next the teacher reinforces that touching each object is a useful strategy to ensure that each object is counted only once. Then the teacher asks the student if they think this is a useful strategy to use all of the time. The teacher might say, "When is it useful to touch each object as you count? Is it useful with any number of objects?" Finally, the teacher invites the child to explore when this strategy is useful and to share their findings with their classmates.	Daily

Conversations for Assessment

I'd like to introduce you to a teacher from Austin, Texas, named Jessica Kellog. Jessica is a kindergarten teacher who has graciously invited me into her classroom on several occasions during math time. Each time I step inside the classroom door I see students gathered around tables, some sitting and some standing. Students are working with math manipulatives and talking and listening to one another. Jessica moves around the room kneeling beside students, talking to them and listening intently to their ideas. As I enter the room on this day, I see the same flurry of activity and engagement that I always do. Jessica is carrying a clipboard with her, and she appears to be taking notes while talking with a group of students. The children are gathered around a large pile of connecting cubes. "Look, I can make a tower," one of the students says as he carefully snaps several of the cubes together and tries to balance it on the table.

Another student says, "Look, look, I made a tower. Mine is the biggest!"

"Wow. David," Jessica comments. "How many cubes do you have?" She carefully watches as David touches each cube, "One, two, four, five, six, eight. I have eight!"

Jessica smiles and says, "David, you kept track of the cubes by touching each one as you counted."

Carlos jumps in, pointing to each cube in the tower; "One, two, three, four, five, six. He has six." Carlos seems proud of his counting, and I wonder how David is feeling about this and how Jessica will respond.

Without skipping a beat, Jessica says, "Carlos, you made a useful decision as a mathematician. You counted again to be sure that we counted correctly. Working together as mathematicians is really important."

After listening to this exchange, I have so many questions for Jessica, and I am excited to have the opportunity to talk with her during her planning period.

After Jessica takes her class to music, we meet back in her room to discuss her conversation with David and Carlos. I am so curious that I begin asking her questions before she can even sit down. "What were you writing in your notes?" I ask. Jessica explains that her goal on this particular day was to gather information about her students' counting development. She explains that one-to-one correspondence (the ability to count each object in a set once) and cardinality (knowing that the last number used to count a set represents the total amount in the group) are examples of skills that she was looking for. Jessica shares her notes with me and explains that Carlos demonstrated one-to-one correspondence and cardinality with the six connecting cubes. She also noted that David touched each item as he counted, which is a strength, and that he is still developing stable order, or the ability to know the name for each number and say them in a sequential order every time he counts.

Jessica's conversations with her students help her to gather data that describe her kindergarteners' counting development. This is ongoing work that enables her to assess what her students know and understand and what skills and concepts they are still developing. Jessica uses this information to design future learning experiences that meet her students' needs. Although these conversations for assessment differ in purpose from math conferences, Jessica will be able to use the data from these counting assessment conversations to guide her future math conferences with students.

Conversations to Scaffold Learning

After visiting Jessica's classroom, I head upstairs to visit a second-grade classroom. The teacher, Jared Paul, is interested in learning more about conferring today. I am visiting to introduce myself as a member of the district's math department and to get to know his class a little bit before our coaching begins. As I enter his classroom, I realize I am a few minutes early and that Jared has not yet taken his students to lunch. It takes just a few seconds for me to be thankful that I arrived early. When Jared sees me, he waves for me to come in from across the room. Jared's students appear to be playing math games. I can see tables full of manipulatives, some with dice and others with spinners. The room is filled with chatter, laughter, and excitement. It doesn't seem like anyone is eagerly awaiting lunch; instead, I suspect there will be groans of disappointment when Jared asks them to clean up.

After taking a few more steps inside the room, I notice a group of students with connecting cubes and piles of brightly colored shoelaces. As I move closer to their table, I can see that one girl has chosen a hot pink shoelace and is straightening it out on the table in front of her. A boy is lining up the connecting cubes below the pink shoelace. Then they repeat this process with a dark green shoelace. Next, the two second graders count the cubes out loud and begin writing something in their notebooks. I don't want to interrupt them, but I am so curious. I kneel down beside them and introduce myself. The girl tells me her name is Jaime, and she seems eager to tell me what they are doing. "We are adding the shoelaces up!" she explains. "We first measure them with the cubes and then we add them up." As Jaime shows me her notebook, I can hear a bit of Jared's conversation at the next table. I thank Jaime for sharing her work with me and then quickly scoot over to listen in on Jared's conversation. He is talking with two students who are working on a very similar activity, except these students are using connecting cubes to measure pieces of yarn instead of shoelaces. As I listen in, I can hear Jared suggest that they try some of the longer pieces of yarn. The children eagerly agree to give it a try, but within a few minutes Jared announces that it is time to clean up for lunch. As I expected, there are loud groans; the kids were clearly enjoying this important work.

Moments later, Jared comes back to the room after dropping his students off in the lunchroom. The purpose of my visit is to talk about conferring, but I hope Jared won't mind me asking a few questions about his conversation with the two boys working with the yarn. Jared shares that his decision to offer the students a longer piece of yarn was intentional. They were ready to work with larger numbers. Jared explains that there are times when his students need a nudge to attempt something more challenging. He knew Felix and Jorge were ready and wanted to encourage them to extend their understanding of counting and measuring to larger numbers. He suspected that with larger numbers, they might begin to discover efficient strategies for counting.

What Jared described is a conversation to scaffold learning. As Jared explained, these types of conversations are intentional and tailored to students' needs. These interactions are important because they help teachers to adjust or modify the learning experience for their students to ensure that they are working within their zones of proximal development. These conversations can also work to reduce students' cognitive load. While productive struggle is useful in mathematics, extreme frustration is counterproductive. These important conversations are a great way to meet the needs of our learners in the moment.

While conversations to scaffold learning and to maintain awareness of students' mathematical development are important components of mathematics instruction, they differ from conferences in their purposes and outcomes. Conferences are an integral part of our math instruction, giving us opportunities to understand our students' thinking, nudge students forward, and foster a thriving community of confident mathematicians.

Chapter 2

The Similarities and Differences between Math and Literacy Conferences

Have you ever observed another teacher and felt so inspired that you raced back to your classroom to make immediate changes? Several years ago, I had an experience like this when I was working as a fifth-grade teacher. I was given the opportunity to observe a fellow teacher during her writing workshop, an area in which I really wanted to grow. Specifically, I had heard a lot about writing conferences and wanted to see one in action.

On this particular afternoon, I remember feeling excited as I stepped into the classroom with four other teachers and our instructional coach. The teacher, Deb Tijerina, was sitting in a rocking chair in the middle of the room with her third-grade students gathered around her on the carpet. As we quietly inched closer to listen in, our instructional coach leaned over and shared that Deb was finishing up her minilesson. When the lesson came to a close, the students moved back to their seats and took out their writing folders and notebooks. Everyone seemed to know what to do and how to get started. After quickly greeting our group, Deb grabbed a small white stool and a binder and sat down beside one of her students. We gathered around to watch, and we heard the following exchange:

DEB: Hi Eric. What are you working on today?

ERIC: I am still writing my story about my skateboard.

DEB: Oh, I am so excited! I had hoped you would keep writing about that. I'm eager to read more about some of those skateboard tricks. Some of them seem really challenging.

ERIC: Yes, they are. I practice every day.

DEB: Wow! You sound really committed. Last time we met you were writing about a very specific day when you went to the skatepark with your dad. Are you still writing about that day?

ERIC: Yeah. I am writing about this one time that I fell. I got hurt pretty badly and then later my dad got me knee pads and elbow pads. I already had a helmet, but I scraped my knees that day. It really hurt.

DEB: This sounds like an important story to tell. Can you read me a little bit from that part?

ERIC: Sure. *I was doing a trick called an ollie, and that went well. Next, I tried to skate down a small ramp. I don't have that at my house, so I wasn't used to it. I fell. I was upset and wanted to go home. My dad took me home.* That is all I have so far from that part.

DEB: Can I tell you something I'm noticing about you as a writer? You do a really nice job of giving the reader the important details they need to understand the order of the events. By using the transition word *next*, you helped the reader keep track of what happened. Using transition words was an important choice and one that I think will really help your readers.

One of the things that I have in my mind is a picture of what I think happened. When you told me the story, I pictured a skatepark that I have been to before. Sometimes readers do this if the author doesn't describe the scene. I wonder though, what if your reader hasn't been to a skatepark? Hmm . . . I wonder if they might have trouble visualizing the park and the ramp.

ERIC: Yeah. My mom said she had never been to one before. When she came one time, she thought it was cool.

DEB: I wonder if there is a way to take your readers to the skatepark! We can't take them in the way you took your mom, but could you use your words to take them there?

ERIC: Maybe.

DEB: One thing writers do is to go back and reread their writing and look for places to add descriptive language. That means language that describes how something looked, smelled, felt, or even tasted. Do you remember our minilesson on adding descriptive language?

ERIC: Kind of.

DEB: [*opens up her binder to the "anchor chart" tab*] Do you remember this anchor chart we created as a class? [*pulls out a small photocopied version of the original anchor chart and places it on Eric's desk*]

ERIC: Oh yeah.

DEB: We talked about some steps authors might take to add descriptive language into their writing. Do you think you could give this a try in this paragraph?

ERIC: Yes.

DEB: Great. I can't wait to read what you come up with! I will leave this anchor chart here with you in case you need it.

The details of this conference have never faded from my memory. At first, I thought it stayed fresh in my mind because I wanted so badly to be able to duplicate that experience with my fifth graders. I admired the conversational tone of Deb's voice when she talked to Eric. And I was equally inspired by how she moved through that conference in a way that appeared unplanned and effortless, yet I knew better. This wasn't an off-the-cuff conversation. Deb went through each of the components of conferring that I had read about: research, decide, and teach (Anderson 2000). Specifically, she listened to Eric to learn more about where he was in the writing process and what he was doing as a writer (research). Then, she thought about what Eric might learn next as a writer (decide), and finally she delivered a very specific and accessible teaching point (teach).

In the years that followed, I conferred with readers and writers until it felt natural. I took comfort in knowing that there was a process or series of predictable steps that supported me when conferring with students. Most importantly, I kept that memory of Deb's conference in my mind, and in particular the way she spoke to Eric as a capable writer. Let's take a look at the specific teaching moves Deb made during the conference and why they were important to growing Eric's writing identity (**Table 2.1**).

Chapter 2 The Similarities and Differences Between Math and Literacy Conferences

TABLE 2.1

Deb's Teaching Moves When Conferring with Writers

What Deb Said	The Move	Why It Is Important
"What are you working on today?"	Research	Deb isn't coming to the conference with a predetermined agenda. Rather, Deb wants Eric to take the lead. She is listening to understand what Eric is working on, thereby reinforcing his identity as a writer who is capable of deciding what to focus on.
"Can you read me a little bit from that part?"	Decide	While Deb listens to Eric's story, she is thinking about his next steps as a writer. She considers both his writing and what he has said to her during the conversation as she chooses a single teaching point that will help move him forward as a writer. Deb is not looking for a long list of things to "fix," nor is she positioning herself as the one with all the answers.
"As a writer, you do a really nice job of giving the reader important details they need to understand the order of events."	Reinforce	Deb reinforces a specific skill or writing move to ensure that the conference starts from Eric's strengths. She explicitly names the writing move so that it is clear to the student. This reinforcement helps Eric gain awareness about what he has done well as a writer while also communicating that he is capable.
"One thing writers do is to go back and re-read their writing and look for places to add descriptive language. Do you remember the anchor chart we created in class? We talked about the steps authors take to add descriptive language into their writing. Do you think you could give this a try in this paragraph?"	Teach	Deb provides one teaching point that is focused and accessible to the writer. This teaching point is not specific to just this piece of writing, but rather this is a generative skill that Eric can use today and in the future. Deb is strategic in her words and tone. She offers a suggestion to the writer, gives him support for that work, and invites him to try it out. Again, Deb's language communicates respect for Eric as a writer and acknowledges that this is his story, and his next steps are his own decision.

Comparing Writing and Math Conferences

If you're a literacy teacher, then you might be hoping that there are some connections between conferring with writers and mathematicians. There are! Many of the teaching moves Deb used in her writing conference also support mathematicians. Both writing and math conferences involve deep listening and observation work. They also share the same overarching goals of supporting students' long-term growth and helping students to develop a love and appreciation for the craft of writing and mathematics. And while literacy and math conferences do have some similarities there are also some important differences. Let's take a look at the comparison chart in **Table 2.2**.

16   Part 1   Math Conferences: What Are They?

TABLE 2.2

Comparing Writing and Mathematics Conferences

Writers	Mathematicians
\multicolumn{2}{c}{The purpose of the conference is to grow the learner, not to perfect the piece or get students to answer a problem correctly.}
\multicolumn{2}{c}{The teacher asks questions to elicit students' thinking.}
\multicolumn{2}{c}{The teacher observes, names, and reinforces a specific mathematical or writing decision.}
\multicolumn{2}{c}{The teacher nudges students in ways that deepen their understanding and provide opportunities for students to share with the classroom community.}
The teacher may teach or model a particular strategy and ask the student to give it a try.	The teacher encourages students to problem solve and reason to determine strategy choice and deepen understanding.
The teacher may encourage the student to study a completed example (mentor text) and extend an invitation to imitate.	The teacher may encourage students to collaborate to share different strategies and ideas and decide when and how they are useful.
Often the teacher confers privately with one student who is working independently.	Often the teacher confers with students that are working collaboratively, enabling the teacher to assign competence publicly.

Teaching the Learner Rather than the Assignment

In *The Art of Teaching Writing*, Lucy Calkins first gave her famous advice, "we are teaching the writer and not the writing" (1994, 228). The first time I read these words, I cringed because I knew I had been doing the latter. I had been focused on helping students to edit or perfect their writing pieces rather than giving them teaching points that would support their growth as writers. As a result, much of my work with students was more as their editor than as a writing teacher. As math teachers, we share a similar goal of growing mathematicians rather than teaching students how to quickly and correctly solve specific types of problems. But what does it mean to grow a mathematician or a writer? Let's think back to Deb's conference. You might have noticed that she didn't edit Eric's work. You may have even been surprised that she never attempted to read his entire story. She began by looking for strengths and then selected a teaching point tailored to Eric's needs as a writer rather than what she thought was needed to correct his writing. Similarly in math conferences, we focus on supporting students by listening and considering their needs as mathematicians while fostering their ability to make connections between mathematical contexts and strategies.

Chapter 2   The Similarities and Differences Between Math and Literacy Conferences

Reinforcing Students' Identities and Abilities

Deb also supported Eric by listening intently to his story about skateboarding, which communicated to Eric that he is a writer with interesting work to share. Although it seemed effortless, Deb was purposeful in her decision to position Eric as the expert of his story, and rightfully so! In math conferences, we can support our students' math identities in a similar way by listening with curiosity and interest as they share their thinking. Most importantly, we can enter the conferences as fellow mathematicians and position our students as the experts of their mathematical work.

Deb also acknowledged Eric's ability to carefully craft a story with important details that help his readers to understand the order of events. Every math and writing conference gives us opportunities like this to provide students with positive, timely, and specific feedback. This feedback serves two purposes. First, it names students' mathematical and writing decisions so that they become transparent and explicit. Our students make decisions each day as mathematicians and writers, and a critical part of our work as teachers is highlighting these decisions as important and worthwhile. Secondly, this feedback reinforces students' strengths, which signals to students that they are capable and competent with useful ideas to share.

Step-by-Step Procedures and Direct Modeling during a Conference

One memorable moment in Deb's conference was when she handed Eric a small photocopy of an anchor chart (**Figure 2.1**). This anchor chart, first presented to Eric in a writing minilesson, gave him clear steps for adding descriptive language to his story.

These types of explicit steps are useful for supporting writers with specific writing strategies and techniques, but they are not as useful for mathematicians during a math conference. In a writing conference, anchor charts like this one do not take the creativity away from the writer. For example, if Eric chooses to use the process outlined in the chart, he still has big decisions to make. He needs to decide which parts of his writing might be enhanced with descriptive language. Next, he will use his five senses to develop that descriptive language all on his own. The anchor chart and the steps guide him, but he will produce a piece of writing that is still uniquely his own. In other words, even if several students in the class utilize this anchor chart, their writing pieces will still most certainly be different.

Anchor charts or notes like these presented to students during a math conference have an entirely different result, one in which the creativity and joy of doing mathematics is reduced. When students are given a method to solve a problem by a teacher, few creative decisions are left. Students end up producing the same work as their peers and have little left about which to talk to one another. If this prescribing of strategies happens often, students might begin to see math as a series of predetermined steps to remember rather than interesting problems that can be solved using multiple strategies.

FIGURE 2.1

Deb's anchor chart for adding descriptive language to a story

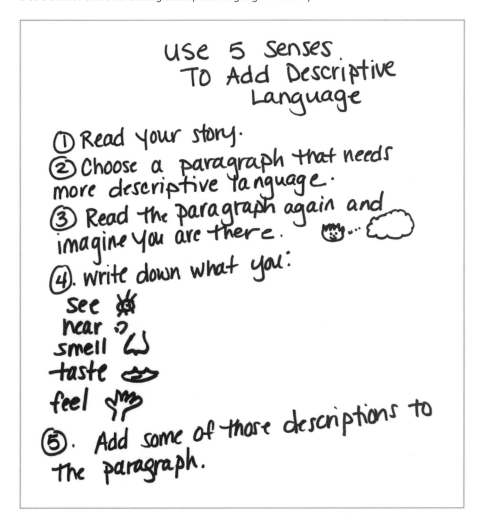

Does this mean that we should never show students how to use a strategy or procedure? No, not at all. In fact, we might encourage students to refer to the work and ideas of their peers that have been highlighted in classroom anchor charts in order to point out strategies they might like to try. We might even ask students to check out what another group is doing to get some ideas. The catch is that we don't want to present students with a list of steps while they are engaged in problem solving because the moment we do this, we have taken ownership of the problem and the only role left for them is to follow the procedure. Our goal is to support students' mathematical thinking while keeping the decision making, creativity, and ownership in our students' hands. Let's consider who owns the mathematics in two hypothetical conferences between a teacher and two first-grade students (**Table 2.3**).

TABLE 2.3

Comparing the Flow of Mathematical Ownership

Conference Version 1	Who Owns the Math?	Conference Version 2	Who Owns the Math?
Teacher: What are you working on? **Student One:** I am trying to figure out what to do. **Teacher:** When I walked up, I saw that you and your partner were sorting the shapes.	Students	**Teacher:** What are you working on? **Student One:** I am trying to figure out what to do. **Teacher:** When I walked up, I saw that you and your partner were sorting the shapes.	Students
Student Two: We just don't know what to do. **Teacher:** Well, there are many ways that you can sort these shapes. Why don't you try sorting them into groups based on the number of sides they have?	Teacher	**Student Two:** We just don't know what to do. **Teacher:** Well, there are a bunch of different shapes here. As mathematicians you get to decide how you'd like to sort them. When I walked up, what were you noticing?	Students
Student Two: Okay.	Teacher	**Student Two:** Some are squares. **Teacher:** What attributes helped you decide that they are squares?	Students
		Student Two: They have four sides. **Student One:** They have corners like this. This one [*holding up a non-square rhombus*] doesn't have the same kind of corners. **Teacher:** Oh, good eye. Those corners are different. I wonder if what you noticed about these shapes and their corners might help you decide how to sort the shapes. I hope you will share what you noticed about the corners of these shapes. I think the class might be interested in hearing your thoughts about the types of corners that squares have.	Students

20 Part 1 Math Conferences: What Are They?

While it might seem easier and more direct to give students the information they need during a conference, what our students really need is a supportive mathematics community that promotes a lifelong love of discovery and problem solving. In order to be mathematicians, students need to engage in the work of mathematicians which includes critical thinking, investigation, creative decision making, and collaboration. In other words, our students need opportunities to engage in the active learning of mathematics. As Tracy Zager shares in *Becoming the Math Teacher You Wish You'd Had*, "A cautious, fearful, obedient, or passive mathematician will not be a mathematician for long" (2017, 53). This prescriptive way of teaching lacks opportunities for students to experience the excitement and joy of learning mathematics. And if you are like me and have taught math in a more direct manner in the past, then you know it takes some of the joy out of teaching mathematics too. Let's reflect on the two conferences presented in **Table 2.3**. How did you feel as you read each one? Could you feel the difference between the children agreeing to complete the math task in the first conference and the children trying out their identities as mathematicians in the second conference? I am hard-pressed to think of anything more rewarding than watching students discover that the world of mathematics isn't something they need to earn their way into. They already belong in this world, and sometimes we get the honor of watching them walk in.

Chapter 3
Types of Math Conferences

Have you ever walked away from a conversation with a group of students and felt like absolutely nothing was accomplished? This has happened to me many times over the course of my teaching career. In fact, there were times when I wondered if my conversations confused my students more than they helped them. Over the years I learned that my most successful conferences were the ones in which I kept my focus on two important goals.

The Goals of a Math Conference	
Goal 1	Understanding students' ideas and interactions
Goal 2	Nudging students toward deeper mathematical understanding and increased engagement within the math community

Although there are different types of math conferences that differ in structure, they all share these same overarching goals. Let's take a look at how Dana Ruiz, a fourth-grade teacher, keeps these goals in mind as she confers with her student, Zoe.

Introducing Zoe

Zoe is an outgoing fourth-grade student who loves every opportunity to work in groups. As you can imagine, her favorite part of math is working collaboratively with her friends, but her teacher, Dana Ruiz, has noticed a change in Zoe over the last few days. Usually, Zoe shares her thinking freely, but ever since the class started working with division problems that have remainders, Zoe has taken on the role of an observer within her group. Dana is eager to confer with Zoe and her group today to observe their interactions and to uncover Zoe's thinking about quotients that include remainders.

FIGURE 3.1

Trevor orders the division problems by dividend from greatest to least

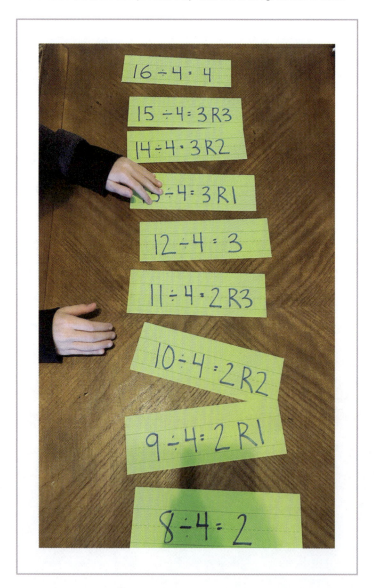

Conferring with Zoe

As Dana approaches Zoe, Kali, and Trevor, she sees that Trevor has taken a set of nine division equations out of a baggie and placed them face up on the table. Dana has instructed the students to work collaboratively to put the division equations in an order that makes sense to them.

Trevor appears to take the lead. "I think we should organize them by the first number. The first number has an order."

The other students seem content with Trevor's plan, and they watch him position the equations, one below the other, ordering the dividends from greatest to least (**Figure 3.1**).

"Why did you decide to order the equations this way?" Dana asks.

Trevor responds casually, "I just noticed that the first numbers go in an order and the second number is always four."

"I see. So, you noticed the divisor in each equation is four," Dana clarifies, "And that the dividends are different."

Hoping to draw Zoe into the conversation, Dana adds, "I'd like to hear from others in the group. What else do you see here that is interesting?"

"Well, some have remainders, and some don't. Is that what you mean?" Kali responds cautiously.

"I think that is a great observation," Dana offers. "As mathematicians there are no right or wrong things to notice. What else do you notice?"

"The remainders start at three and then get smaller and then it starts over," Zoe shares.

"Tell us more about your thinking," Dana suggests.

"Well, the remainders keep going: three, two, one, and no remainder, which is kind of weird," Zoe shares with a giggle.

Goal One of the Conference: Understanding Students' Ideas and Interactions

So far in the conference, Dana has kept her focus on learning more about her students' mathematical thinking as well as how they are interacting as members of a group. Using the information she gathered in the moment through questioning and observation as well as her prior knowledge about her students, Dana responded in ways that she believed would further uncover their thinking and attend to the uneven participation. Let's take a closer look at what Dana observed and how she responded (**Table 3.1**).

TABLE 3.1

Debriefing Dana's Conference with Zoe and Her Group

What Did Dana Observe?	What Does Dana Know?	How Did Dana Respond?	Why Did She Respond That Way?
Dana noticed that Trevor had taken the lead.	Dana has noticed that Trevor's peers perceive him to be a strong mathematician. It is not uncommon to see students letting Trevor take the lead, even if the material is new to him.	Dana asks Trevor questions about his decisions so that his thinking becomes transparent to the group. Next, she follows up with questions that invite others to share their thinking.	Dana knows that working on tasks collaboratively within a mixed-ability group is important, but she also knows that the best learning occurs when all group members participate and share their ideas. Dana wants each member of the group to see value both in sharing their ideas and listening to the ideas of their peers.
Kali shared her thinking but seemed cautious.	Kali doesn't often take the lead in math tasks, but she usually shares her thinking when she suspects her group is making a mistake.	Dana listens to Kali's mathematical thinking and affirms her decision to share her observation.	Dana wants to encourage Kali and her group to make mathematical observations and to see their ideas as important.
Zoe had not yet shared her thinking.	Zoe is not normally this quiet and is rarely cautious in sharing ideas even if she hasn't had time to think them through.	Dana asks what else the group notices.	Although Dana did not specify that this question was for Zoe, Dana suspected that Zoe had an idea to share. Dana wanted to give Zoe another opportunity to share her thinking.

Goal Two of the Conference: Nudging Students toward Deeper Mathematical Understanding and Increased Engagement with the Math Community

At this point in the conference, Dana wants to nudge students toward deeper mathematical understanding and discovery. Dana noted that Zoe and Kali were initially reluctant to share their thinking and had just begun to share their ideas. Dana intends to nudge the students to engage more deeply with this task. She hopes that with encouragement they will discover additional patterns and connect those patterns to their understanding of dividends, divisors, and remainders.

Additionally, Dana intends to encourage the group to engage with the math community and begin to think about sharing their discoveries and ideas with the rest of their classmates. Let's listen in and see how Dana confers with these goals in mind.

The Conclusion of Zoe's Conference

"You have all done some really important work," Dana affirms. "Mathematics is about discovering and understanding patterns, and you have pointed out some really interesting patterns. We have some other groups that are working with different equations, but I am wondering if they have noticed any of the same patterns. Would you consider looking for more patterns and then sharing them with our math community today? I think everyone will be interested in what you have discovered and what these patterns might mean."

Two Types of Math Conferences

FIGURE 3.2
Two structures for mathematics conferences

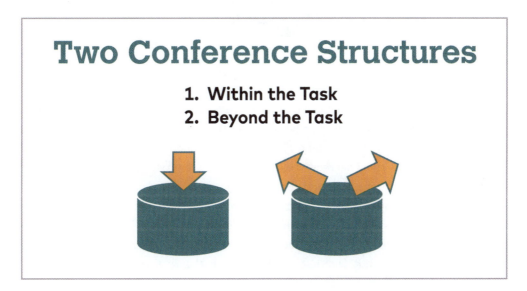

As you might have guessed, Dana's decision to engage students in this math activity was intentional and based on her students' needs. Over the last few days, Dana had observed that many students in her class needed more time to grapple with the concept of remainders in order to understand how they connect to divisors and dividends. Just as Dana selects math tasks with her students' needs in mind, she is also intentional about how to nudge students' thinking during a math conference. After talking with Zoe, Kali, and Trevor, Dana made the important decision to confer *Within the Task* rather than *Beyond the Task*. This means that she nudged the students to continue to explore the remainders using this particular task rather than encouraging them to consider how the mathematics might work in other contexts or in different types of problems. But what exactly does it mean to confer *Within the Task* as compared to *Beyond the Task* (**Figure 3.2**), and why might you choose one over the other?

Conferring *Within the Task*

FIGURE 3.3
Within the Task conference structure

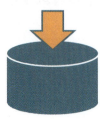

As you read the conversation between Dana and her students, you might have noticed that Dana didn't direct her students toward noticing anything in particular. For example, she didn't guide them to notice that the remainder was never more than three or ask them to consider why the remainder decreased by one as the dividend decreased by one and then went back to three. The instructional decision to give her students the time and space to notice and make their own observations was intentional. Dana knew that observing, noticing, and making sense of mathematical patterns is challenging yet important work for her students. She also observed that Zoe and her groupmates had not yet considered these patterns in depth, nor had they begun to explain why they occur. This is precisely the reason that Dana selected a *Within the Task* structure (**Figure 3.3**). She wanted to nudge her students to notice the patterns within this specific task rather than ask them to make generalizations about remainders. She suspected that they might develop a deeper understanding of division concepts if they had more time to consider the patterns within these particular division equations.

A *Within the Task* conferring structure has four distinct parts: (1) notice and understand, (2) uncover student thinking, (3) name and reinforce, and (4) invite sharing. Let's take a closer look at these four parts and analyze them within the context of Dana's conference with Zoe, Trevor, and Kali.

Within the Task Conferring Structure

Dana moved fluidly through each of the four parts of a *Within the Task* conference, from noticing and understanding what her students were working on and how they were working together, to uncovering their mathematical thinking, to naming and reinforcing a specific mathematical decision and then finally inviting them to share with the math community. Let's study this conference a bit more by identifying each component and its purpose (**Table 3.2**).

TABLE 3.2

Components of a *Within the Task* Conference and Their Purposes

Component of the Conference	What Dana Said or Did	Purpose of the Component
Notice and Understand	Dana approached Zoe and her group as they were working collaboratively and observed them.	When we approach a group of students with the primary intention of listening and observing, we ensure that students maintain ownership of their work. Observing and listening closely to our students positions us to confer from where students are in their understanding.
Uncover Students' Thinking	Dana asks, "Why did you decide to order the equations this way?"	At this point in the conference, it is helpful to ask questions to understand how students are thinking about the mathematics. While we may be able to see what students have done, these questions are focused on eliciting more information about how and why students made particular mathematical decisions. This information is critical to understanding the connections students are making between mathematics concepts and how they are generalizing mathematical ideas.
Name and Reinforce	Dana explains, "Mathematics is about discovering and understanding patterns, and you have pointed out some really interesting patterns."	After uncovering students' thinking, it is helpful to select a mathematical decision made by the group and name it explicitly. Naming the decision increases students' awareness of how their choices support them as mathematicians and encourages them to continue this work now and in other contexts.
Invite Sharing	Dana asks, "Would you consider looking for more patterns and then sharing them with our math community today?	In the final moments of this type of conference, it is important to invite the students to share their thinking with the math community, thereby reinforcing their identities as valued mathematicians with important ideas to share. Additionally, this invitation reminds students that the center of this work is the math community rather than the teacher.

Dana decided to confer *Within the Task* after the conference began. She needed to understand her students' thinking and ideas before she could decide how to nudge them forward in their work. Let's look at another conference that Dana had on the same day as students were working on the same task. In this case, Dana decided to confer *Beyond the Task* (**Figure 3.4**). As you read, see if you can spot the moment that Dana decided to use this conference structure.

Conferring *Beyond the Task* with Terrance and Arnav

FIGURE 3.4
Beyond the Task conference structure

Dana isn't surprised to see Terrance working with Arnav. The two boys are great friends and seem to jump at any chance to work together. Dana has noticed that Terrance and Arnav often finish tasks quickly. They seem confident in their mathematical abilities and sometimes need to be nudged to think deeply and make connections between mathematical concepts. Dana wonders how Terrance and Arnav will approach this task, especially since there aren't any answers to calculate. She hopes this task will give her an opportunity to uncover their thinking and to help them deepen their understanding of division concepts.

As Dana walks up alongside the two students, she sees that they have placed their division equations one above the other on the table (**Figure 3.5**). Dana notices that they have ordered the division equations from greatest to least dividend, just like Zoe's group (**Figure 3.1**).

FIGURE 3.5

Arnav pointing to the equations without remainders

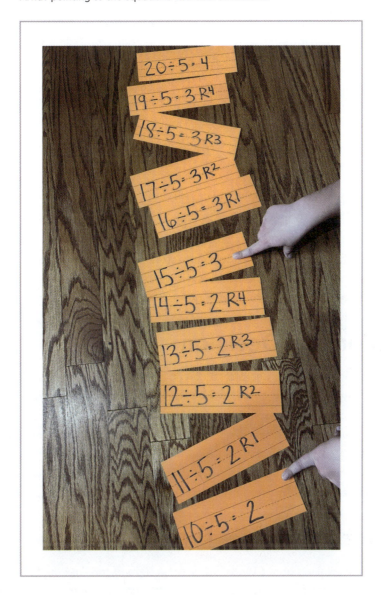

"I see you have the equations placed in an order. Can you tell me about this work?" Dana asks.

"I noticed that they are all dividing by the same number, so I put them in the order of the first number," Terrance offers.

"Yeah, it was pretty easy," Arnav says with a smile.

"So, you noticed right away that the divisor in each equation is five?" Dana paraphrases.

"Yes," Terrance interjects, "And that the dividend decreases by one for each equation. Then you can see here," Terrance says, pointing to the cards, "The remainders decrease four, three, two, one."

"It goes to zero too. I mean, the remainders go four, three, two, one, then none. That's because these equations, right here," Arnav says, pointing to the equations without remainders, "they divide evenly by five."

Chapter 3   Types of Math Conferences   31

"Did you notice anything else?" Dana nudges, hoping to elicit more thinking.

"Well, it's not something I noticed," Terrance says, seemingly unsure if he should share his thoughts. "It's just something I think. I'm pretty sure the remainders start at four because there can't be a remainder of five. If there is a remainder of five, then you could have divided again."

"You did some really challenging work here today. You noticed patterns and then you attempted to explain them mathematically. Terrance and Arnav, I'd like you to think more about this. If you are correct, this is a big mathematical idea. Terrance, are you saying that equations like these, with a divisor of five, can never have a remainder other than four, three, two or one?

"They can't. It wouldn't make sense," Terrance shares, sounding even more confident than before.

"I agree with Terrance," Arnav says. "If you have a remainder that is the same as what you are dividing by, then you made a mistake."

"This is a really big idea. It sounds like you are saying this might be true for all division problems. If so, I think you have an interesting idea for a conjecture here. Why don't you work on gathering some evidence to learn more about when and how it works, and then drafting a conjecture. I think our math community is going to find this really interesting."

In-The-Moment Decision

Could you spot the moment Dana decided to confer *Beyond the Task*? Dana did a lot of careful questioning in the beginning of this conference to really get under Terrance and Arnav's thinking. When Terrance shared his idea about why it made sense to him that none of the remainders was greater than four, Dana had a hunch they were on the cusp of generalizing about the relationship between divisors and remainders. She wanted them to continue this inquiry-centered work. Similar to a *Within the Task* conference, Dana nudged the students to work as self-directed mathematicians and ensured that they remained the owners of their ideas.

Mathematical Conjectures

Before we move on to thinking about the structure of a *Beyond the Task* conference, let's dig into what we mean by the term *conjecture* and how Dana's students seemed familiar with creating them. Setting up the math community is essential to having productive math conferences in which both teacher and students know what to expect. As part of this process, students and teachers become familiar with creating conjectures, which are mathematical hypotheses that the students believe to be true but have not yet proven. Often conjectures develop from the patterns that students notice within a problem or across problems. In action, this looks like students using a particular math task or problem as a starting point and then moving beyond that specific problem or context to look for larger mathematical truths (Zager, 2017).

Conjectures don't need to be original to math communities outside the classroom walls; rather, they are new to *our* students and *our* classroom community. For example, while many adults understand that 5 + 4 = 4 + 5 and that changing the order of the addends will not result in different sums, this will likely be a new and exciting discovery for students in primary grades. Conjectures are our students' new mathematical ideas and theories and are a starting point for further discussion and analysis. Just as we see in Terrance and Arnav's conjecture (**Figure 3.6**), conjectures can help students go beyond any single math problem to understand the structure and ideas behind it.

FIGURE 3.6

Trevor and Arnav's conjecture and evidence ("*The remainder for any division problem will always be less than the divisor.*")

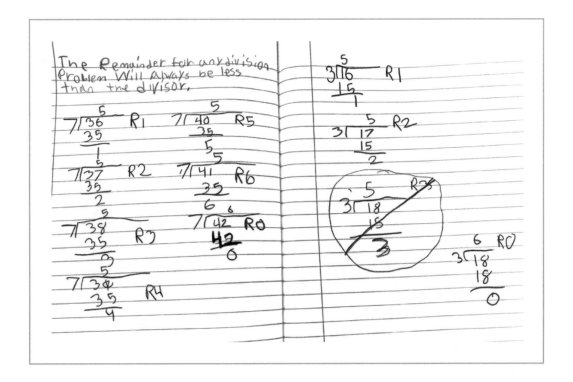

Beyond the Task Conferring Structure

As you listened to the conference between Dana, Arnav, and Trevor, did you notice similarities between this conference and the *Within the Task* conference? *Beyond the Task* and *Within the Task* conferences share some of the same components, yet they differ in how students are nudged forward in their work.

Both of Dana's conferences began with noticing and understanding, followed by asking questions to uncover students' thinking. Dana's decision to opt for a *Beyond the Task* conference was an in-the-moment decision based on what she believed would be the best way to deepen her students' understanding of division and remainders. Although Dana noted that Arnav and Trevor were confident mathematicians, her decision to confer *Beyond the Task* was not based on their abilities. Both types of conferences require our students to reason and think deeply about the mathematics. Rather than students' abilities, the decision about which conference to select is based on what you believe the students need at that moment in order to grow as mathematicians. This means deciding whether students would benefit more from further exploration of the mathematics within the current math task or problem or whether they would benefit from exploring the mathematics in other contexts to make broader mathematical generalizations. Let's take another look at this conference and the purpose for each of the components (**Table 3.3**).

Chapter 3   Types of Math Conferences   **33**

TABLE 3.3

Components of a *Beyond the Task* Conference and Their Purposes

Component of the Conference	What Dana Said or Did	Purpose of the Component
Notice and Understand	"Can you tell me about this work?"	When we approach a group of students with the goal of listening and observing, we ensure that students maintain ownership of their work. Observing and listening closely to our students positions us to confer from where students are in their understanding.
Uncover Student Thinking	"Can you tell me about your thinking?" "So, you noticed right away that the divisor in each equation is five?" "Did you notice anything else?"	At this point in the conference, it is helpful to ask questions to understand how students are thinking about the mathematics. While we may be able to see what students have done, these questions are focused on eliciting more information about how and why students made particular mathematical decisions. This information is critical to understanding the connections students are making between mathematics concepts and if and how they are generalizing mathematical ideas.
Name and Reinforce	"You noticed patterns and then you attempted to explain them mathematically."	After uncovering students' thinking, it is helpful to select one of the group's mathematical decisions and name it explicitly. Naming the decision increases students' awareness of how their choices support them as mathematicians and encourages them to continue this work now and in other contexts.
Nudge Thinking Beyond the Task	"Are you saying that equations like these, with a divisor of five, can never have a remainder other than four, three, two or one?" "It sounds like you're saying this might be true for all division equations."	This is the moment that the teacher decides to nudge the students beyond the current math task. The goal is for students to make generalizations about the mathematics that can be applied to other contexts and equations.
Invite Conjecture and Sharing	"I think you have an interesting idea for a conjecture here. Why don't you work on gathering some evidence to learn more about when and how it works, and then drafting a conjecture. I think our math community is going to find this really interesting."	In the final moments of the conference, students are encouraged to develop and share their original ideas and work with the classroom math community. This helps to reinforce their positions as valued members of the community, crafting their work for their peers rather than the teacher.

Deciding Which Conference to Select

When reading about the components of conferences, or any pedagogical strategy for that matter, it is easy to initially think of them as a set of rigid steps to follow. But conferring is anything but rigid! Conferring is, above all, a listening practice and our next steps are always guided by the students in front of us. So, while the components of a conference are there to support our conversations and give them a predictable flow, we can never know the exact direction a conference will go in until we are in it. Therefore, deciding which type of conference to use is a decision that we make during the conference by using the information gathered in the moment. Although we can't plan our conference in advance, there are some things that we can listen for to aid in the decision-making process (**Table 3.4**).

TABLE 3.4

Look-Fors to Help Select the Conference Structure

You might select a *Within the Task* conference if you notice...	You might select a *Beyond the Task* conference if you notice...
students grappling with how the mathematics works within the given math task. **Example:** Two fourth-grade students solved a subtraction problem. One solved using the standard algorithm and the other student used base ten blocks to model their thinking. Both students can solve subtraction problems but have not yet made connections between the computations in the standard algorithm and their understanding of place value.	*students explaining how mathematics works in this particular problem but have not yet considered if or how it might work in other contexts.* **Example:** Two first graders joined two addends in different orders and got the same sum. After conferring with them, you suspect that they think this is a coincidence.
students have made a mathematical decision while working on the current task, and you want them to think more about why this decision was useful and to share it with the math community. **Example:** A group of first-grade students are measuring the length of classroom objects with their shoes. They decide to use the same shoe each time because someone in the group noticed that different sizes of shoes were resulting in different measurements.	*students are starting to make generalizations.* **Example:** While conferring with a group of fifth graders, they explain that "multiplying something by one half is the same as finding half of the other number." After talking more with the group, you believe they would benefit from exploring this idea further by finding evidence and examples that extend beyond this particular problem.
students discovered something important that is directly related to this math task. **Example:** A group of third graders are working with arrays to represent multiplication and announce excitedly that you can find a sixes fact by doubling a threes fact. While you know that this thinking can be extended beyond multiplication facts for threes and sixes, you feel they would benefit from exploring these two types of facts further, creating additional visuals, and then sharing their thinking with the class.	*students seem to have stumbled upon a useful strategy or decision that you would like them to explore beyond the current problem.* **Example:** Two kindergarteners are counting objects. One stops and appears to notice that his counting doesn't sound right. The student stops counting and starts over and begins to count again. While conferring with the students, you think they would benefit from thinking about this decision as an important strategy for keeping track of their counting. You would like to encourage them to explore when this recounting strategy might be useful for mathematicians.

Chapter 3 Types of Math Conferences

In education it sometimes feels like there are right and wrong ways of doing things. We worry that we might have made the wrong decision in the moment. And while it is always a good idea to reflect on our instructional decisions, we should remember that there is not one right way to confer, and we can never predict exactly how a conference will go. Students surprise us every day with their unique perspectives, ideas, and ways of thinking about mathematics. That being said, the more we confer, the more we find ourselves in familiar territory, and the better prepared we feel for the conversations. Perhaps we begin to see similarities in the ways students engage with a particular task, or maybe we become so familiar with a mathematics concept that we come to the conference with predictions about the types of connections students might make. The conference components themselves are also there to provide us with some level of predictability to the flow of the conference. But our decisions about whether to nudge students to deepen their understanding *within* the current task or to nudge them to generalize *beyond* the task will always be an authentic, in-the-moment decision. And either conferring structure, *Beyond the Task* or *Within the Task*, will support our mathematicians by ensuring that they maintain agency and ownership of their work and view themselves and their classmates as important contributors to mathematical knowledge and understanding.

Chapter 3 Types of Math Conferences

Part 2

Effective Questioning:

What Types of Questions Elicit Students' Thinking?

Chapter 4

Questioning to Promote Thinking and Understanding

Have you ever been right in the middle of a lesson and already know you are going to do it differently next time? These in-the-moment reflections are powerful, not only because we know what we want to improve but because we already have ideas about how we will do it. But have you ever had an experience when you weren't sure? As a fifth-grade teacher, I remember feeling this way every time I asked my students a series of questions. I could sense that I was doing the heavy lifting in the conversation and perhaps directing my students' ideas rather than listening to them, but I wasn't sure why this was happening. Were my questions the problem, or was I just asking too many questions? Or maybe I wasn't giving my students enough time to think before asking a follow-up question. Let's visit my old fifth-grade classroom and take a closer look.

My Fifth-Grade Classroom

As you enter my classroom, you'll see my students gathered on the carpet for the community share. Caris and Brian are presenting their work to the class under the document camera. Caris is explaining how she and Brian approached a math task that involved multiplying fractions (**Figures 4.1** and **4.2**). At this point in the year, my students had experience adding and subtracting fractions, but multiplying fractions with whole numbers was a new concept. I was excited to see how my students might approach this problem and hoped that they would use their understanding of whole number multiplication to develop strategies to multiply a whole number and a fraction. Let's listen in on the questions that I asked my students and to the way my students responded.

FIGURE 4.1

Apartment Mulch Math Task

An apartment complex near our school refreshes the outdoor space each spring. They put $16\frac{1}{8}$ pounds of mulch around each tree.

There are 16 trees in the apartment complex.

How many pounds of mulch do they need to buy?

FIGURE 4.2

Caris and Brian's work showing how they began solving $16\frac{1}{8} \times 16$ by using their understanding of the distributive property to multiply 16×16 first

$$16\frac{1}{8} \times 16$$

$$16 \times 16 \qquad 16 \times \frac{1}{8}$$

$$16 \times 10 \ + \ 16 \times 6$$

$$10 \times 6 = 60$$

$$160 \qquad 6 \times 6 = 36$$

$$160 + 60 + 36 =$$
$$100 + 120 + 36$$
$$220 + 36$$
$$256$$

Questioning Caris and Brian

"So, at first, we knew that the apartment building has 16 trees that need mulch," Caris explained. "We also knew that each tree needs 16 1/8 pounds of mulch. We knew we needed to multiply 16 1/8 by the 16 trees. Next, we broke 16 1/8 into 16 + 1/8 and wanted to multiply 16 × 16 and 16 × 1/8. We multiplied 16 × 16 and got 256 (**Figure 4.2**). That's as far as we got."

"Did you and Brian come up with any ideas about what to do next?" I asked.

"Umm, I'm actually confused about how to multiply the fraction," Brian said. "My brother taught me how to multiply something by 1/2, but I wasn't sure about 1/8."

"What if the problem was 16 × 2, instead of 16 × 1/8. What would you do then?" I nudged, hoping Caris and Brian would draw on their understanding of multiplication with whole numbers.

"I would just double 16," Brian responded, seeming a bit surprised by my question.

"Why would you double 16?" I asked.

This time Caris responded. "Because if you multiply something by 2, you can double the groups."

"Ahh," I said, feeling like we were getting somewhere. "So, multiplying has something to do with groups?" Since a few seconds went by and Caris and Brian did not respond to my question, I tried again. "How many groups would you make to solve 16 × 2?"

"You could make 2 groups of 16 or 16 groups of 2," Caris responded matter-of-factly.

"So, if you want to multiply 1/8 × 16, could you make groups?" I prompted.

"Oh yeah, Brian said. "You could make 16 groups of 1/8."

"I have Cuisenaire rods here," I offered. "Can someone come up and create a model that represents 16 groups of 1/8?"

"I can," said Amy. "When we used these before, the brown was the whole and the white ones were eighths. So, if you take 16 of the white ones and you put them all together you have 2 wholes" (**Figure 4.3**).

FIGURE 4.3

Amy uses Cuisenaire rods as a model for 1/8 × 16

Funneling Students' Thinking and Ideas

Could you tell which strategy I wanted my students to use? You might have noticed that my questions directed Caris and Brian to solve 16 × ⅛ by adding equal groups of ⅛. This type of questioning is called funneling. "The funneling pattern of questioning involves using a set of questions to lead students to a desired procedure or conclusion, while giving limited attention to student responses that veer from the desired path" (National Council of Teachers of Mathematics, 2014, 37). By using this type of questioning, my entire class was guided safely toward the correct answer. While it might be true that their understanding of this particular strategy was deepened by Amy's model with Cuisenaire rods, funneling comes at a cost. Take a look at some of the possible unintended results of funneling (**Table 4.1**).

TABLE 4.1

Asking Questions That Funnel Student Thinking

Intended Result	Unintended Result
Helping students. Sometimes we ask leading questions because we want to provide instructional support.	**Significantly reducing or eliminating the cognitive demand required in a task.** Questions that funnel student thinking take away almost all of the decision making, reducing the task to a series of steps for students to follow.
Encouraging success. It can be hard to watch students struggle. Sometimes we offer a series of questions to guide students in the "right" direction so that they can answer the question correctly and feel successful.	**Sending false messages about the purpose of mathematics.** All mathematicians struggle and sometimes problems take a lot of time to figure out. Productive struggle isn't a bad thing, nor is it something we should try to rush along or eliminate. Without opportunities to grapple with complex ideas, students may begin to see mathematical uncertainty as academic inability and develop negative beliefs about themselves as mathematicians. Additionally, when nudged consistently toward one method, students may not experience the creativity which is inherent in mathematics.
Being Responsive. We know that strong teachers are responsive to their students' needs. Sometimes we ask questions that funnel students' thinking because we are aware of our students' misconceptions and believe our role is to quickly intervene.	**Facilitating dependent learning.** Directed questioning that leads to a specific method or strategy may cause students to lose their sense of agency. After several experiences like this, students may try to figure out what the teacher wants them to do rather than reason mathematically for themselves. This can lead to students becoming dependent rather than independent mathematicians. Dependent mathematicians focus on what they believe the teacher wants them to do. Independent mathematicians understand there are many possible strategies, and each way of thinking about the mathematics deepens their understanding of the concept.

You might be wondering how I felt after questioning Caris and Brian as they shared their mathematical thinking. I felt the way I always did: exhausted! This type of questioning is a lot of work for the teacher. I felt enormous pressure to figure out what strategies would make the most sense to my students, and then guide them down a path that I thought would ensure success. I resorted to funneling as soon as Brian mentioned he wasn't sure how to multiply the fraction by the whole number. I responded with, "What if the problem was 16 × 2, instead of 16 × ⅛. What would you do then?" In this moment, it became clear to Brian, Caris, and the rest of the class that I had a specific method in mind. Let's take a look at a possible scenario that might have unfolded if I hadn't asked that question and instead took a different approach.

Share Out with Caris and Brian, Take Two

GINA (TEACHER): Did you and Brian come up with any ideas about what to do next?

BRIAN: Umm, I'm actually confused about how to multiply the fraction. My brother taught me how to multiply something by ½, but I wasn't sure about ⅛.

GINA: Yes, we have a lot of experience multiplying whole numbers. This is a new challenge for us. Tell me more about what you are thinking.

BRIAN: I mean, one thing I have been thinking about is how I know how to multiply things by ½. My brother taught me that when you multiply something by ½ that you just take ½ of the other number. So ½ × 10 is 5. I was thinking about that when I was trying to figure out what to do next.

GINA: Let's record that on the board. [*writes ½ × 10 = 5*] This is important and we will want to think more about your brother's idea. Does anyone have anything to ask or to add to what Brian has shared?

CARLOS: I do. [*looks down at his fingers*] I think his brother is right because I added ½ ten times and got 5.

GINA: You added ½ five times just now?

CARLOS: Yes, I sort of did it with my hands. I can show you. Every two fingers is one whole because each finger is ½. If I put them together, I have five wholes.

GINA: Carlos, can you record this thinking on the board next to the equation ½ × 10 = 5?

CARLOS: Sure. [*Carlos comes to the board and draws a visual representation of solving ½ × 10 by adding ½ ten times*]

GINA: Carlos, can you explain your thinking?

CARLOS: So, I thought of half of something and then I thought of having ten of them. So, if I had ten groups of that, it would be five wholes. So, like half of a candy bar. Then if I had ten of those, I could put the halves together.

GINA: How does this compare to what Brian's brother said? Brian, can you explain again what your brother said?

BRIAN: He might be wrong, but he said that ½ × 10 is the same as ½ of 10, which is also 5.

GINA: Hmm, Brian's brother and Carlos got the same answer, but they have two different explanations. Let's write down what Brian's brother said. [*writes on the board ½ of 10*] Does anyone want to share their thinking about how or if these ideas connect with one another?

TANYA: My group did what Carlos did. We made 16 groups of ⅛. I don't think Brian's brother is wrong, but I don't really understand that strategy.

I pause for a few moments of silence to see if anyone wants to add to this idea, and then I say, "I am going to take our thinking from the whiteboard and record it on chart paper. These ideas are important, and we will want to revisit them. We will have more time to explore multiplying fractions with whole numbers tomorrow. Let's go back to our seats and reflect on our work today. On a sticky note, answer this question: Which way of thinking about ½ × 10 makes the most sense to you and why?"

What Could Have Been

Wouldn't it be nice if we could go back in time like this and redo our teaching, carefully crafting each question? Of course, I can't know for sure if Brian, Caris, or Carlos would have responded in exactly this way, but I do know that the way I funneled their thinking in our fifth-grade classroom left little room for them to share their own thoughts and ideas. Did you notice that this second time around I was okay with ending the lesson without an agreed upon answer? Not only did my questions change in this version, but my intended purpose changed. My goal wasn't to get them to the correct answer as quickly as possible, nor was my goal tied to this particular math task. This change in focus helped me to reframe my questions.

Mathematical Thinking Outside of the Classroom

As I think back on that day in my fifth-grade classroom, I know that I felt nervous when Brian began talking about what his brother had taught him. I remember that Brian used to mention his big brother often in class. Brian's brother seemed to love teaching him new mathematics skills. Feeling nervous was a direct result of my belief that I needed to be in control of the conversation and particularly in control of what strategies my students were exposed to. Not only did this belief about my role as the teacher lead me to funnel and overdirect students' thinking, it may also have given my students the impression that mathematics sits within the four walls of our classroom. Brian was connecting his learning to things he had grappled with at home with a family member. Moments like these, when our students share their experiences with mathematics outside of school, should be celebrated so that our students understand that mathematics exists in every space. I suspect that by navigating the class away from Brian's experience, I might have communicated the incorrect message that the mathematics we were doing in class was somehow different or separate from the mathematical conversations and experiences they were having outside our classroom.

Our Purpose for Asking Questions Guides Our Questions

I wish I could say that once I learned about funneling questions, I never used them again. Truthfully, this has been a hard habit to break. These types of questions sneak into our conversations at precisely the moment that our purpose for questioning shifts from developing students' understanding to guiding them toward the answer. Our students can often sense this shift which sends conflicting messages about the nature of mathematics and our perceptions about their abilities as mathematicians. Funneling questions might also surface when we feel rushed or worried that students don't have enough instructional time to meet their learning goals. Although instructional time is always scarce, developing our students' mathematical thinking will always be time well spent. The foundation they take with them to middle school may be the foundation they build on for the rest of their lives. This is a stance I wish I had taken back then. So, although I didn't quite know how to improve my questioning, I now realize that it wasn't that I needed to learn to ask better questions, but rather that I needed to reflect on my purpose for asking my students questions in the first place.

Chapter 5

Selecting Questions for Specific Purposes

Have you ever been in someone's classroom and found yourself wishing you could stay all day? That is how I feel when I am in Katie Chrischna's kindergarten classroom. Katie's enthusiasm for teaching rubs off on everyone around her, including her students. Although I worked in the role of instructional coach in Katie's classroom, I'm certain that I learned more about teaching kindergarten from her than she did from me.

Katie and I shared a passion for teaching math, and we loved reading articles and books about teaching mathematics. We often discussed new strategies that we had read about, and then we'd try them out together in her classroom. One of the topics we spent a great deal of time learning about was conferring and specifically questioning during conferences. Recently, a principal asked me if I could take a group of math teachers to observe a teacher who is strong at questioning. I knew instantly that I would ask Katie if she'd be up for a visit.

Before the observation, I met with the teachers to share a couple of documents that Katie and I always found useful for questioning. First, I shared the question types developed by the National Council of Teachers of Mathematics (NCTM) in their book *Principles to Actions* (NCTM, 2014) (**Table 5.1**). Each of the question categories is named by its purpose: Gathering Information, Probing Thinking, Making the Mathematics Visible, and Encouraging Reflection and Justification. Although there are four question types, Katie and I found that we rarely used Gathering Information questions during conferring. Although there may be times when this type of question is needed, we noticed that Gathering Information questions typically yield only one specific answer and are more useful during conversations for assessment.

I also shared a Questioning Support Document for Math Conferences (**Table 5.2**) that Katie and I used to align question types to the moment in the conference in which they would most likely be asked. My hope was that as we observed Katie, the visiting teachers might be able to use these documents to identify the types of questions Katie was asking and to notice when Katie was using specific question types during the conference.

TABLE 5.1

Question Types from *Principles to Actions: Ensuring Mathematical Success for All* (NCTM, 2014)

Question Type	Description
Gathering Information	Students recall facts, definitions, or procedures.
Probing Thinking	Students explain, elaborate, or clarify their thinking, including articulating the steps in solution methods or completion of a task.
Making the Mathematics Visible	Students discuss mathematical structures and make connections among mathematical ideas and relationships.
Encouraging Reflection and Justification	Students reveal deeper understanding of their reasoning and actions, including making an argument for the validity of their work.

TABLE 5.2

Questioning Support Document for Math Conferences

Conferring Component	Question Type You Might Use	Some Examples
Notice and Understand	Probing Thinking	• What are you working on?
Uncover Student Thinking	Probing Thinking	• Can you tell me about your thinking? • What were you thinking when you made that decision?
	Making the Mathematics Visible	• How does this visual represent your thinking? • How did you use this model in your work?
Name and Reinforce	None (Teacher notices and names a group's strategy and mathematical decision rather than using questioning in this component.)	
Invite Sharing (*Within the Task*)	Making the Mathematics Visible	• Another mathematician in our class has created a different visual representation. Can the two of you share and compare your representations? • As you share your thinking with the class today, can you share a representation or model to help explain your mathematical ideas?
	Encouraging Reflection and Justification	• As you share your thinking with the class today, can you give examples to help explain your mathematical ideas?
Nudge Beyond the Task (*Beyond the Task*)	Encouraging Reflection and Justification	• When does this work? • When does this *not* work? • Why does this work? • When is this useful?
Invite Conjecture (*Beyond the Task*)	Encouraging Reflection and Justification	• Can you develop a conjecture along with examples and non-examples to share with the class?
	Making the Mathematics Visible	• What visual representations or models can you create to help explain your conjecture?

Katie's Conference with James and Kenny

Upon entering Katie's room, the visiting teachers and I noticed the students gathered in a large circle on the floor in front of Katie. We could hear the students taking turns saying numbers in a counting sequence: "16, 17, 18, 19, 20." As we stepped in closer, we could see that as each student said a number, they pushed one connecting cube to the center of the circle. After the last student said their number and added their cube, Katie asked, "So, how many cubes are in the circle?"

As students shared their thinking, we noticed that a few students were unsure how many cubes were in the circle at the end of the count. Katie, with all her experience, didn't appear surprised by this. Knowing Katie, I assumed she was taking mental notes on which kids might still be grappling with cardinality and which students demonstrated understanding of this counting principle in this particular moment. After showing genuine interest in their ideas, Katie asked for suggestions on how they might know for sure. Of course, the only way to resolve the issue was to count them again, which Katie's students seemed eager to do!

A few minutes later, we watched as Katie asked the students to select a math activity from several bins already placed on the tables throughout the classroom. When most students had made a decision and started working, Katie grabbed her rolling chair and sat down next to two students, James and Kenny. As Katie watched the two students, I leaned over to the teachers and explained that Katie was in the Noticing and Understanding portion of the conference. At that moment, Katie was watching Kenny and James to get an idea of what they were working on. James and Kenny didn't stop working when Katie sat beside them. I suspected that this was because the students in Katie's class were used to her sitting beside them and observing them while they worked.

At their table, James and Kenny each had their own ten-frame in front of them along with a shared pile of red and yellow counters and a stack of cards. James flipped over the first card, which revealed the numeral five and five dots. Both boys placed five counters on their ten-frame, filling up the bottom row. Next, Kenny flipped over a card with the numeral eight and eight dots. Kenny touched the last counter in his row of five and said, "Five, six, seven, eight." As he counted "six, seven, eight," he touched three of the empty places on his ten-frame. Then he placed three counters into those empty spots. James looked down at his ten-frame and put three more counters on. Then James touched his counters and said, "Five, six, seven, eight" (**Figure 5.1**).

FIGURE 5.1

James placing 5 counters on his ten-frame

After James had finished his counting, Katie moved a little closer to the pair of students and began to speak.

KATIE: What are you working on today?

JAMES: We are doing our ten-frame.

KATIE: I saw you both touching the counters while you were counting. Why were you doing that?

JAMES: We were touching them to count them to make the number on the card.

KATIE: I see the card shows eight. I saw you touch the counters and says *five, six, seven, eight*. Why did you start at five?

KENNY: Because there were already five counters filled in.

KATIE: Can you show me what you mean?

JAMES: When this part is filled up (pointing to the bottom row of the ten-frame), that means there are five.

KATIE: I think I understand. So, do you mean that when this bottom row is filled up, you don't need to count them?

KENNY: No, you just know.

JAMES: See look, *one, two, three, four, five* (touching each counter in the bottom row as he counts).

KATIE: This is really important work. You noticed that five counters were already filled in and you counted on from five to eight. During our community share, would you feel comfortable sharing your work with the ten-frame? I think your fellow mathematicians would be really interested in how you are counting on using your ten-frame to make larger numbers.

Debriefing the Conference Type

After observing a few more conferences, the teachers and I made our way to the school's conference room. We had about thirty minutes before Katie would join us to debrief our visit. Although the teachers had observed a few different conferences while in Katie's room, they immediately began talking about the conference with James and Kenny. While we waited, I thought it might be worthwhile for us to listen to the audio recording that I had taken of this conference and see if we could identify the type of conference Katie had chosen. As we listened, we noted that Katie never asked the students to work on something other than the card task with the ten-frames. Although we could sense that Kenny and James were beginning to make generalizations about counting on, Katie guided them to continue to explore this concept using the task that they were already working on. We also noted that Katie didn't ask James and Kenny to develop a conjecture. For these reasons, we believed that Katie had conducted a *Within the Task* conference, and we were eager to ask her about this decision. Next, we listened to the conference several times while I scripted it out to help us identify each component (**Table 5.3**).

TABLE 5.3

Katie's *Within the Task* Conference with James and Kenny

Within the Task Kindergarten Conference

Conference Component	Conference Transcript
Notice and Understand	*Katie watches the students engage in the task for a few minutes before speaking.* **KATIE:** What are you working on today? **JAMES:** We are doing our ten-frame.
Uncover Student Thinking	**KATIE:** I saw you both touching the counters while you were counting. Why were you doing that? **JAMES:** We were touching them to count them to make the number on the card. **KATIE:** I see the card shows eight. I saw you touch the counters and say *five, six, seven, eight*. Why did you start at five? **KENNY:** Because there were already five counters filled in. **KATIE:** Can you show me what you mean? **JAMES:** When this part is filled up (pointing to the bottom row of the ten-frame), that means there are five. **KATIE:** I think I understand. So, do you mean that when this bottom row is filled up, you don't need to count them? **KENNY:** No, you just know. **JAMES:** See look, *one, two, three, four, five* (touching each one as he counts).
Name and Reinforce	**KATIE:** This is really important work. You noticed that five counters were already filled in and you counted on from five to eight.
Invite Sharing	**KATIE:** During our community share, would you feel comfortable sharing your work with the ten-frame? I think your fellow mathematicians would be really interested in how you are counting on using your ten-frame to make larger numbers.

Debriefing the Conference Type with Katie

Although the main purpose of visiting with Katie was to observe her questioning techniques, the teachers were eager to know more about why Katie had made the decision to confer *Within the Task* with James and Kenny. As Katie entered the room, the teachers quickly began asking her about the conference with Kenny and James. Katie shared that even though she has been conferring for years, she still has moments of questioning what to do next! She said that during this conference she felt that Kenny and James would benefit from continued exploration of numbers using this task because, based on this conference and other observations, she hasn't witnessed Kenny or James counting on from numbers other than five.

She said, "I also haven't observed how Kenny and James might make a smaller number on their ten-frame. For example, if they drew a five next, would they clear the frame and make the smaller number, or would they remove three counters? I felt that this task provided James and Kenny with the opportunity to think about the idea of hierarchical inclusion [knowing that all numbers that precede a given number are included within that number] as well as how numbers within ten relate to each other."

Katie admitted that as she reflected on her conference, she could also see benefits in asking Kenny and James to move *Beyond the Task* to make generalizations about counting on. She said, "I could envision a future conference in which I ask Kenny and James to generate their own numbers to think about when and how counting on is beneficial for mathematicians. But in this moment, I decided to confer *Within the Task* because I felt that additional opportunities to make numbers within ten would deepen their understanding of hierarchical inclusion and that this task was a great way for Kenny and James to continue to explore this concept.

Debriefing the Questions with Katie

Next, the teachers were anxious to hear how Katie selected the questions that she asked Kenny and James. Katie shared that when she first started conferring, she often felt unsure about what questions to ask next. She explained that the NCTM question types really helped with this uncertainty. Instead of trying to remember specific questions on the spot, she thought about what she wanted to know at that particular moment in the conference. Let's take a look at the table in **Figure 5.2** for ideas about the type of information we might want to elicit from students at each point in the conference.

FIGURE 5.2
Information elicited from students during conferences

Information Elicited from Students during *Within the Task* and *Beyond the Task* Conferences
Both types of conference begin with the same components.

Conference Component	Information We Might Want to Elicit from Students
Notice and Understand	• What are the students working on? • How are they engaging in the work? Are they working alone or collaboratively? • Are they in the middle of their work or are they just getting started? • Do they seem confused or unsure of how to start? • If they are working collaboratively, are any students taking the lead? • Which students are talking and sharing? • What tools are they using? • Have they created any models or visual representations?
Uncover Students' Thinking	• Why have they made specific mathematical decisions? • What connections are they making between mathematical concepts and prior knowledge? • Do they understand what they have written down or what the group is working on? • How are they connecting the model or representation that they have made to the mathematics? • Are they thinking *Beyond the Task*? Are they making generalizations?
Naming and Reinforcing	None as this is a time for naming students' strengths rather than eliciting information.

The teacher chooses whether to confer *Within the Task* or *Beyond the Task*

Part 2 Effective Questioning: What Types of Questions Elicit Students' Thinking?

Within the Task Conference

Information Elicited from Students During a *Within the Task* Conference

If you want to engage in a *Within the Task* conference, you'll shift to inviting sharing after naming and reinforcing.

Conference Component	Information We Might Want to Elicit from Students
Invite Sharing	• Would the students feel comfortable sharing their ideas with the classroom math community? • Would the students feel comfortable sharing their ideas with another student or group of students? • Can the students create a visual representation to describe the mathematics?

Beyond the Task Conference

Information Elicited from Students During a *Beyond the Task* Conference

If you want to engage in a *Beyond the Task* conference, you'll shift to nudging beyond the task after naming and reinforcing.

Conference Component	Information We Might Want to Elicit from Students
Nudge *Beyond the Task*	• What do the students know about how and when this particular strategy or mathematical idea works? • What questions do the students have about how this idea connects to other mathematical ideas and contexts?
Invite Conjecture	• Would the students feel comfortable coming up with a conjecture to describe their generalization? • Would the students like to investigate examples and non-examples to support their thinking? • Would the students see value in creating visuals to support their mathematical thinking? • Would the students like to engage in further collaboration?

To further their understanding, the teachers used the transcript of Katie's conference to analyze Katie's questions. With Katie's support, they thought about each question that Katie asked and her purpose for asking it. Let's look at the chart in **Table 5.4** for a deeper analysis of the question types that Katie used during her conference with James and Kenny.

TABLE 5.4

Katie's *Within in the Task* conference transcript labeled with NCTM question types and conference components

Within the Task Kindergarten Conference Tagged with NCTM Question Types

Conference Component	Conference Transcript
Notice and Understand	**KATIE:** What are you working on today? *(Probing Question)* **JAMES:** We are doing our ten-frames.
Uncover Student Thinking	**KATIE:** I saw you both touching the counters while you were counting. Why were you doing that? *(Probing Question)* **JAMES:** We were touching them to count them to make the number on the card. **KATIE:** I see the card shows eight. I saw you touch the counters and say *five, six, seven, eight.* Why did you start at five? *(Probing Question)* **KENNY:** Because there were already five counters filled in. **KATIE:** Can you show me what you mean? *(Making the Mathematics Visible)* **JAMES:** When this part is filled up (pointing to the bottom row of the ten-frame), that means there are five. **KATIE:** I think I understand. So, do you mean that when this bottom row is filled up, you don't need to count them? *(Making the Mathematics Visible)* **KENNY:** No, you just know. **JAMES:** See look, *one, two, three, four, five* (touching each one as he counts).
Name and Reinforce	**KATIE:** This is really important work. You noticed that five counters were already filled in and you counted on from five to seven.
Invite Sharing	**KATIE:** During our community share, would you feel comfortable sharing your work with the ten-frame? *(Making the Mathematics Visible and Inviting and Encouraging Reflection and Justification)* I think your fellow mathematicians would be really interested in how you are counting on using your ten-frame to make bigger numbers.

Improving Your Questioning

Observing an experienced questioner like Katie can be exciting, but at times it can also feel overwhelming. Although Katie mentioned moments of uncertainty herself after the conference, in the moment she seemed calm and confident. It is easy to watch other teachers and think they have it all figured out. I do this frequently! It helps to remind myself that no teacher can predict exactly what a student will say or do during a conference. And wouldn't it be boring if we could! Your questions don't need to be planned ahead of time, and you shouldn't feel pressure to know what you will ask before sitting beside your students. Rather than trying to plan the actual questions, try using Katie's method of thinking about the information that you'd like to elicit from students at that moment in the conference. Think about what you could ask to uncover their thinking or to make the mathematics visible. When you keep your focus on what you want to know, different questions will emerge. This way of questioning leads to authentic conversations that will feel natural for you and your students. If you get off track, don't panic. Stop and think about what you really want to know and try again. The best part of conferring is that as it becomes a consistent practice within your classroom, you will likely find that there are specific questions you use often. You'll also find that many conferences will offer an opportunity to ask something new!

Part 3

Asset-Based Conferring:

How Does Focusing on Students' Strengths Support Them in Making Conjectures?

Chapter 6

Conferring from Students' Strengths

My first year as a teacher was one of my favorite teaching experiences. I worked in a small neighborhood school in Illinois that was built in 1951. My classroom had so much charm and character. I remember the windows that actually opened and lined the back wall of the classroom, giving us all the opportunity to see every person as they walked up to the school! Unlike many newer classrooms, this classroom had a door that was made of dark, solid wood and was chipped in some places, showing its age. This dark wood was carried throughout the classroom, from the built-in bookshelves to the trim that lined the windows. And the final bit of charm came from the large, green chalkboard placed on the front wall. Although whiteboards were a welcome gift in future years, I have such happy memories of those fall mornings teaching at the chalkboard with the cool breeze drifting through the windows.

As a new teacher, I had my hands full with thirty-four first graders. I didn't know a whole lot about teaching math, but I was eager to be the best possible teacher for my students. That year I spent countless hours working in my classroom after school. I would sift through students' work and do my best to assess their understanding in order to make instructional decisions. Although I loved teaching, this part of the job left me feeling tired and overwhelmed. It seemed like my students had so many misconceptions and partial understandings. I wanted to support my students, but sometimes I felt like I was climbing a mountain that was getting taller each day.

Looking back, I don't think I realized how much time I spent looking for students' errors. It never crossed my mind that identifying students' strengths and nudging them forward from those bright spots might be a more effective use of my time. I know that I was doing my best to make decisions based on what I thought I should do and sometimes based on my memory of how my teachers had supported me when I was a student. I think about those days often because it reminds me that sometimes what feels natural or even familiar may not always be the most effective teaching practice.

Years later, as an instructional coach, I wanted to support teachers with the skill of conferring from strengths rather than errors. I was always on the lookout for teachers with strong conferring practices who would be open to letting other teachers observe them. Mitchell Stevens is one such teacher whose authentic appreciation for his third-grade students' mathematical ideas and decisions is apparent from the first day you meet him. Happily for me and the teachers with whom I work, Mitchell is always willing to have visitors come and learn from him and his students. One visit to Mitchell's room really stands out in my memory. On this particular day, Mitchell's principal joined us, and to my surprise, she had concerns about what she observed. Specifically, she noticed that the students with whom Mitchell was conferring had made a pretty big mathematical error. She wanted to know why Mitchell hadn't addressed the error directly with his students. Let's see what happened:

MITCHELL: Today I have a really exciting task for us to work on in groups [**Figure 6.1**]. It is about pizza! You see, there are some kids who have been given different slices of pizza and they think something quite unfair has been done to them. They think their friend got more pizza than they did. In groups, I want you to look at the three scenarios in your slide decks and determine if there is any truth to their claims. Did someone get less pizza in each scenario? If so, who? I am giving you paper, Cuisenaire rods, and fraction tiles that you can use as you work. Be ready to share your findings with the class.

FIGURE 6.1

The opening slide in the The Big Pizza Debate task

Mitchell's students began working on the task in small groups of about four or five. Mitchell walked around the room, listening in on conversations as students looked through the different scenarios on the slide deck. After about five minutes of observing and listening, he approached a group of students and began conferring with them.

MITCHELL: Wow! You all got started really quickly! I see you have folded the paper and colored some of it. Can you tell me about your thinking?

TRISTAN: We are doing this one. [*points to his computer to show which problem his group is working on* (**Figure 6.2**)] We folded the paper to show the sizes of each fraction.

FIGURE 6.2
One of three scenarios in The Big Pizza Debate task

MITCHELL: Tell me more!

JANA: This one shows ⅓ and this one shows ¼ [**Figure 6.3**].

FIGURE 6.3
Jana, Tristan, and Melody's visual representations for comparing ¼ and ⅓

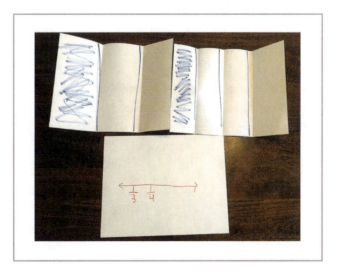

Chapter 6 Conferring from Students' Strengths **65**

MITCHELL: Ahh okay. Tell me more about your decision to make these visuals using folded paper. How did this help you as mathematicians?

JANA: We did it so we could prove that ⅓ is more than ¼. We actually already knew that. But we made these to show it.

MITCHELL: Can someone else in the group explain what Jana means when she says you already knew it?

MELODY: Because a pizza cut into three pieces would make bigger pieces than if it was cut into four pieces. Those would have to be smaller.

MITCHELL: Tell me about this second visual you created. It looks like a number line [**Figure 6.3**].

TRISTAN: We wanted to show it another way too.

MELODY: Yeah, I had the idea. Since we have been putting fractions on the classroom number line, I thought we could also make our own number line for this problem.

MITCHELL: Wow, wow, wowee. Your decision to create two visual representations to show your mathematical thinking and reasoning was an excellent decision. Your fellow mathematicians are going to have an easier time understanding your thinking because you have chosen to show it in more than one way.

I am curious about something you said earlier. You said you just knew one of these unit fractions would be smaller than the other. This seems like the start of a conjecture. Why don't you develop a conjecture that you can test out. It sounds to me like you are saying that the size of a unit fraction has something to do with the denominator. Why don't you all develop a conjecture that really describes what you are thinking.

TRISTAN: Yeah. When it is bigger, the piece is smaller.

MITCHELL: Are you sure? You and your group have some talking and testing out to do!

Noticing and Responding to Students' Errors

Did you spot the error that Mitchell's principal was concerned about? Take a look at the students' number line. Although they verbalized that ⅓ is a larger slice of the large pizza than ¼, their number line does not reflect this thinking. So, why didn't Mitchell address this error during the conference? After the observation, Mitchell shared with his principal that he doesn't point out errors during conferences. Instead, he makes one of two choices: (1) let students continue on their current path, which may lead to the discovery of the error, or (2) guide students to explore the concept in ways that make the math visible.

Addressing Students' Errors during a Conference

Let students continue down their current path, which may lead to discovery of the error.

Guide students to explore the concept in ways that may make the math visible.

Letting Students Continue Down Their Current Path

During Mitchell's conference with Tristan, Jana, and Melody, the three students were reasoning about the relationship between denominators and the size of unit fractions, yet the number line did not reflect this understanding. Was this error related to their understanding of number lines or the size of the unit fractions? In the moment, Mitchell wasn't sure. Yet, he believed that his students demonstrated enough understanding that they would likely discover their number line error as they worked to develop a conjecture around unit fractions. Mitchell also suspected that if they didn't catch this error, their classmates would notice it during the share out. This peer noticing would have the added benefit of being a relevant class discussion because Mitchell has noticed that third graders often make the error of ordering unit fractions on a number line by their denominators.

Guiding Students toward Discovery

While Mitchell was conferring with Tristan, Jana, and Melody, he noticed that they appeared to be reasoning conceptually about the sizes of the fractions in the math task. Not only did the students describe why it made sense to them that ⅓ is a larger slice of pizza than ¼, they also created a model using folded paper that matched their thinking. Although their number line did not represent the ideas they shared during the conference, Mitchell suspected further reasoning might lead them to question the number line they created. But what if the students hadn't shown evidence of thinking conceptually about the sizes of the fractions and instead had only created the number line? Let's take a look to see how Mitchell might have guided them toward discovery of the error by encouraging them to explore the mathematics in a more visual way:

FIGURE 6.4

Jana, Melody, and Tristan's open number line with an error

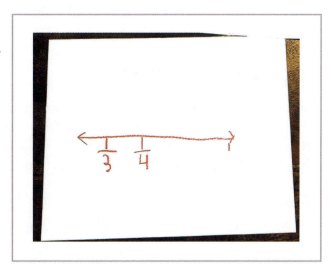

Chapter 6   Conferring from Students' Strengths   **67**

MITCHELL: Wow! It looks like you all got started right away. I see you have drawn a number line here. Can you tell me about this representation [**Figure 6.4**]?

JANA: Yes, we put the fractions on a number line to show which piece of pizza was larger.

MELODY: Yeah, I had the idea. Since we have been putting fractions on the classroom number line, I thought we could also make our own number line for this problem.

MITCHELL: How did this visual representation help you as mathematicians?

TRISTAN: We can see that ¼ comes after ⅓. So it helps us to know that ¼ is the bigger piece of pizza.

MITCHELL: You have done something really important here. You know that fractions are numbers that occupy a specific point on a number line. Using a number line is a great visual representation to help show your thinking about which number is larger and therefore closer to one whole.

I noticed that Kyra and Delany are creating a model of their thinking using fraction tiles. They are using the fraction tiles to represent slices of pizza and trying to figure out what ⅓ and ¼ might look like. Why don't the three of you join Kyra and Delany to share and compare your representations and models. I think it will be really important to show your thinking in multiple ways when you share with the math community.

Debriefing the Conference

In this version of the conference, Mitchell decided to guide his students down a path in which they would have an opportunity to think deeply and visually about the size of each fraction using fraction tiles. Rather than being concerned about whether or not the students' number line error was corrected at that moment, the more important goal is ensuring that students have an opportunity to develop a robust understanding of unit fractions. Through discussing and examining Kyra and Delany's concrete fraction tile model, these students would have an opportunity to reason about the sizes of each slice of pizza and consider how that understanding connects to their number line. This time for collaborative sense making and reasoning work would likely be more meaningful to Mitchell's students than him pointing out the error or explaining the mistake to them.

Starting with Strengths

Knowing how to confer with our students without pointing out every error is an important skill set not only for math teachers but for those teaching other content areas as well. In their book, *One to One: The Art of Conferring with Young Writers*, authors Calkins, Hartman, and White write: "It is easy as a teacher to take hold of someone else's work and to look at it with eagle eyes, searching for flaws we can correct and errors we can fix" (2005, 64). Instead of examining students' work for errors, these authors suggest that we ought to be looking at students' work and saying to ourselves, "What can I gush over?" (Calkins et al. 2005, 64). The same is true for teachers of mathematics. When we give ourselves the permission to listen to our students' thinking and admire their work, we will find no shortage of things to gush over! And those amazing things are what we will name and reinforce during our conferences. This strengths-based approach keeps the flow of our conferences moving in a positive direction and affirms students' mathematical abilities. But what are some of the strengths we might want to name and reinforce? Let's take a look at **Table 6.1** for a few ideas.

TABLE 6.1

Strengths to Name and Reinforce

Collaboration	Students' decisions to work together, share ideas, and provide feedback to one another
Organization	Students' methods and structures for organizing information or keeping track of their ideas
Representations	Students' creation of visual representations and models to make the mathematics visible and deepen their understanding
Generalizations	Students' decisions to look for patterns, notice relationships, and make connections between mathematical ideas
Creative Choices	Students' decisions to try something new, invent a strategy, or attempt to solve a problem in a new way
Disposition	Students trying again after being challenged, exhibiting perseverance and finding the joy in working on difficult problems

Conferring Tools to Help Identify, Name, and Reinforce Students' Strengths

As a teacher I have always loved If-Then charts. When I'm learning a new teaching method or strategy, If-Then charts help me find an entry point and try out a new idea. As I gain more experience with a strategy, I find that I begin to internalize and innovate on the ideas in the charts, and may refer to them less frequently. The If-Then charts in this chapter (and also in Appendix A for easy reference) were created with this process in mind, as supports to help you identify, name, and reinforce students' strengths during a conference. These documents are not all-inclusive because our students do far too many amazing things for them to possibly fit into one chart! My hope is that these charts provide support as you begin to confer with your students, and serve as a list of suggestions rather than a script. We should always remember that conferences are conversations. While you can use these documents to guide you and to feel prepared, the power of conferences is that they are authentic conversations.

TABLE 6.2

Early Numeracy Skills to Name and Reinforce *If/Then*

If the student is...	Then you might say...
touching each object as they count pushing objects together in groups as they count	I noticed that you touched each object as you were counting. Why did you do that? What a great way to keep track while you are counting.
counting a set of objects more than once	I noticed that you counted that set and then counted it again. Why did you do that? I think you are right. Counting again is important to do when the first count doesn't seem right.
suggesting that a fellow mathematician count again or that a count is incorrect	I noticed you suggested that your group should count again. Sharing ideas and giving helpful suggestions is an important part of being a member of a math community.
subitizing and counting on	I noticed that you only touched some counters. You started counting on at _____. Can you tell me more about how you did that? You figured out that counting on can be much more efficient than counting each object one by one.
organizing objects in lines or groups	What an interesting way to organize the objects. Why did you group them like that? The way you organized the counters seems helpful for counting them and noticing which groups have more or less.
estimating	I heard you say that you had more/fewer/the same amount of counters as your last collection even before you started to count. How did you know that? You estimated the number of counters you had and made a reasonable guess. This is a helpful thing to do before counting a collection of objects, so you can know if the amount you count makes sense.
adjusting an estimate	I noticed that you changed your estimate. Why did you do that? Knowing that you can change an estimate when you have new ideas or information is really important.
recording their ideas	What did you write down? What a great way to keep track of your thinking and to share your ideas with others.
counting more than one object at a time	As I was listening, I heard you counting but not by ones. Can you tell me more about your counting? You used a counting pattern to skip count. That is an efficient way to count a collection of objects.
using what is known about one quantity to describe another quantity	How did you know that this collection was more/less than _____? Describing and comparing collections of objects seems like a good way to think about how many you have. Mathematicians can use what they know about one collection to describe another collection.

TABLE 6.2 (continued)

Early Numeracy Skills to Name and Reinforce *If/Then*

If the student is...	Then you might say...
using knowledge of number parts to count, add, or subtract	I notice that you added/subtracted/counted _____. Where did that number come from? What a useful idea. Breaking numbers into smaller parts can be helpful when you are counting/adding/subtracting.
drawing pictures of objects to count, add, or subtract	What did you draw here? Your drawing helps explain what is going on in this problem.
drawing dots or symbols to represent objects to count, add, or subtract	I see you made dots. What are those? What a helpful strategy. Drawing dots instead of _____ is an efficient way to record what is happening.

Chapter 6 Conferring from Students' Strengths

TABLE 6.3

Grades 2–5 Skills to Name and Reinforce *If/Then*

If the student is...	Then you might say...
using the associative property of addition a + b + c = (a + b) + c = a + (b + c)	You mentioned that you grouped these addends together and added them instead of adding the numbers in the order they were listed in the problem. Why did you choose to group the numbers in that way? Using the associative property of addition can help you group and add numbers in ways that make sense to you. This shows your flexibility as a mathematician.
using the associative property of multiplication a × b × c = (a × b) × c = a × (b × c)	You mentioned that you grouped these two factors together and multiplied them instead of multiplying the numbers in the order in which they were listed in the problem. Why did you choose to group the numbers in that way? Using the associative property of multiplication can help you group and multiply numbers in ways that make sense to you. This shows your flexibility as a mathematician.
using the commutative property of addition a + b = b + a	So, are you saying that you thought of this problem as 8 + 2 rather than 2 + 8 because you felt it was easier to think about? Your decision to use the commutative property of addition enabled you to problem solve in a way that made sense to you and was efficient given those numbers. As a mathematician you know how useful it is to think flexibly.
using the commutative property of multiplication a × b = b × a	So, are you saying that you thought of this problem as 0.5 × 50 [rather than 50 × 0.5] because you felt it was easier to think about? Your decision to use the commutative property of multiplication enabled you to problem solve in a way that made sense to you and was efficient given those numbers. As a mathematician you know how useful it is to think flexibly.
using a number sense strategy to add/subtract/multiply/divide	So, you're saying that you [name the strategy the student used]. That strategy seemed to help you add/subtract/multiply/divide.
rethinking their work because something doesn't make sense or isn't reasonable.	You mentioned that you are going to start over/rethink your work because your answer isn't reasonable. This is an important mathematical skill. It is important to stop and think again when something doesn't seem right.
drawing a visual representation/creating a model	Your decision to draw a visual representation/make a model seemed to help you understand the problem. Visuals are an important tool because they help you to understand and communicate ideas.
estimating	So, you estimated first? Estimating is an important skill for mathematicians. It really helps you to know if you are on the right track or if you need to rethink your strategy.

TABLE 6.3 (continued)

Grades 2–5 Skills to Name and Reinforce *If/Then*

If the student is...	Then you might say...
using a second strategy to check their work	So, you are doing it this way just to be sure you get the same results? Using a second strategy is a great way to make sure that your answer is correct. The ability to move flexibly between strategies is a helpful way to check your work so you can communicate correct and precise information.
analyzing a data representation	So, it seems like you analyzed the graph/chart/information before you made any strategy decisions. Taking the time to notice how the data are represented and organized before making quick decisions can help you interpret data representations with accuracy.
connecting previous math knowledge to new mathematical learning	So, you said that you knew _____ and wondered if it would work for _____. You understand how useful it is to actively look for connections between what you are working on and what you already know.

Practicing the Skill of Naming Students' Strengths with Colleagues

Naming and reinforcing students' strengths can be challenging at first, but with time and practice you will find that it begins to feel natural. You will soon begin to observe many of the same strengths and become more comfortable naming those for students. I have found that two great ways of practicing the skill of identifying and naming strengths in a collaborative setting with fellow educators are (1) by using pre-made conferring scenarios cards (**Figure 6.5**) and (2) by analyzing authentic student work samples.

Conferring Scenarios

Conferring scenarios are a great way to practice the skill of identifying students' strengths. You can find a pre-made set of conferring scenarios to use with your colleagues in Appendix B. To use the cards, begin by gathering a small group of educators and the conferring scenario cards that match your grade level. Select one card and read the scenario together. After ensuring that everyone has had enough think time, take turns sharing the strength you might name and what you would say to reinforce this strength if you observed it in a math conference. Not only will this practice help you refine the art of naming and reinforcing students' strengths, but it's also a lot of fun listening to colleagues share the strengths that they noticed. If at first you find yourself focusing on a student's error or misconception, that is okay. Stop and try again. This work is designed to help make assets-based conferring a habit of mind, and habits take time to develop!

FIGURE 6.5
Kindergarten/first-grade example of a conferring scenario card.
Find the full set of conferring cards in Appendix B

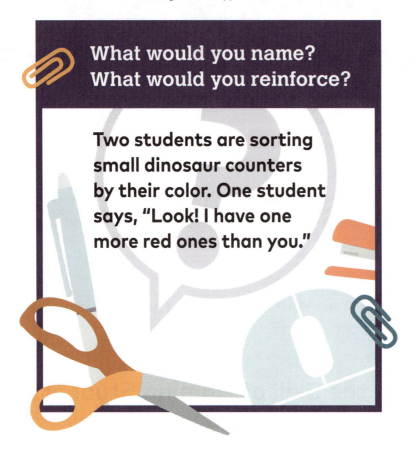

Analyzing Student Work Samples

Analyzing students' work for strengths is another way educators can prepare for conferring from an assets-focused stance. Students do so many amazing things, and it can be an enjoyable process to discuss those strengths together with colleagues. Deep conversation is the focus of these meetings. For this reason, consider discussing just a few samples of student work rather than a bunch of them. Attempting to analyze too many samples can cause the conversation to feel rushed and leave you without enough time to discuss your thinking.

Recently I had the pleasure of joining Mitchell and his team of third-grade teachers as they engaged in the process of analyzing students' work to identify strengths. They decided to each bring a student work sample from a formative assessment they had recently given to their students (**Figure 6.6**). This formative assessment, called *directed paraphrasing*, was designed by Mitchell and his team to gather information about students' understanding of the relationship between the size of a unit fraction and the denominator. Students were given this assignment on a Google Document and were given the option to use virtual or physical math tools. Let's take a look at each student's work and listen in to hear the thinking between the third-grade teachers.

MITCHELL: Alright. I think we are ready to get started. I see we all have our samples here. Just like last time, we will look at each one together. As we do, we will ask ourselves, "What strengths do we notice and what does this student understand?" Let's start with this one here. It belongs to Jackson [**Figure 6.7**].

FIGURE 6.6
Directed paraphrasing formative assessment

> ## Directed Paraphrasing:
> What is the relationship between the denominator of a unit fraction and the size of a unit fraction?
>
> **Who:**
> An adult in your life (mom, dad, aunt, uncle, grandparent)
>
> **What:**
> Explain the relationship between the denominator of a unit fraction and the size of the unit fraction.
>
> **Think About:**
> Be sure to explain words such as *unit fraction* and *denominator*!
>
> **Must Haves:**
> Include words and visual representations to help them understand. You can use these math apps to create visual representations and copy and paste them into this document. Or, you can draw your representations onto this paper.

FIGURE 6.7
Jackson's work using the math app Fraction Tiles from The Math Learning Center (www.mathlearningcenter.org)

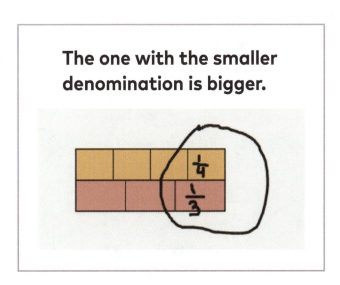

Chapter 6   Conferring from Students' Strengths   75

JAY: I see one strength right away. I am impressed by Jackson's decision to line up the models to show that ⅓ is larger. By lining them up this way he appears to understand that the whole must be the same size when comparing fractions.

MITCHELL: I also think he did a nice job of putting his thinking into words. He explains that he knows the fraction with the smaller denominator is larger.

TINA: I know we should focus on strengths, but I can't help but wish he had written more.

MITCHELL: I feel that way a lot when looking at students' work outside of a conference. That's what makes conferences so great. In the moment, we can ask them questions to really understand their thinking. Given the information we have, what strength would you name for Jackson? What do you hope he will continue to do as a mathematician?

KARLA: Well, I think what you said about how he is referring to the same size whole is pretty important. Considering he wasn't directed to make this representation and he chose his own manipulatives from several options, this seems like a pretty big strength. I think I would name and reinforce that.

TINA: I agree. I might say, "I can see from your model that you used fraction tiles to create two wholes." In an actual conference, I might ask him to tell me about that decision. I'm wondering if he might talk more about how this model enabled him to compare the two wholes because they are lined up and they are the same size and shape. From there I might say, "Your decision to create two wholes of the same size is really important. You understand as a mathematician that when we compare fractions, we need to be sure that we are referring to the same-sized whole. Your visual representation makes this clear to your fellow mathematicians."

KARLA: Let's look at Sydney's next [**Figure 6.8**].

FIGURE 6.8
Sydney's work using the whiteboard app from The Math Learning Center (www.mathlearningcenter.org)

JAY: I really like how she said, "because it has more pieces." To me that seems like a strong level of understanding of how the denominator relates to the whole.

MITCHELL: I was thinking the same thing.

KARLA: I think it is also a strength that she explained the meaning of a unit fraction. It is important that she understands it is one part of a whole that has been partitioned into a certain number of parts.

JAY: I think if I was conferring with Sydney I would want to name and reinforce the use of a visual that matched her thinking. I know that it was required as part of the assignment, but I still think it is important to name that for Sydney. I think that it might be important for Sydney to hear that taking the time to create visuals is worthwhile for mathematicians because it makes their thinking clear to others. As Sydney begins to develop conjectures, she will build off that strength to ensure that she is being precise with her representations, so that her fellow mathematicians are clear about her thinking.

TINA: Should we look at Lili's next [**Figure 6.9**]?

FIGURE 6.9
Lili's work using the virtual whiteboard app from The Math Learning Center (mathlearningcenter.org)

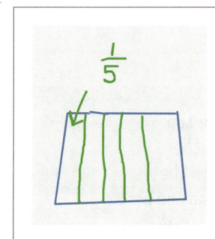

KARLA: First, I love that she took the directed paraphrasing to heart. Her letter format is precious. This is totally Lili!

JAY: Yes, I can hear Lili explaining this to her mom! I think a strength is that she used a real-world context to help make sense of the mathematics.

MITCHELL: Similar to Sydney, Lili's visual matches her explanation. She's also making a connection between the denominator and the total number of pieces or parts in the whole.

KARLA: I agree. Those are both definitely strengths. Although I think we could name either of them, I would probably name the strength of using a real-world context. I think that being able to give context to mathematical ideas is important for mathematicians when they are trying to explain their thinking to the math community.

JAY: Yeah. Sometimes it is hard to decide which strengths to name, and I think either one would be beneficial to Lili.

MITCHELL: Agreed. Sometimes I find myself naming more than one strength. That really isn't as effective as just selecting one. I think it almost lessens the impact of what we are trying to reinforce if we name too many things at once. Naming just one strength keeps the conference focused and direct and gives the student one clear thing to build on.

JAY: Can we look at Zeke's next [**Figure 6.10**]? I brought his because I really struggle with knowing how to confer from strengths if a student might have some misconceptions.

TINA: I have a few students ordering fractions this way too. I see one big strength though. He knows that a unit fraction has a numerator of one. His words also make me think he knows that fractions have something to do with parts of a whole.

FIGURE 6.10
Zeke's work using the whiteboard app from The Math Learning Center (mathlearningcenter.org)

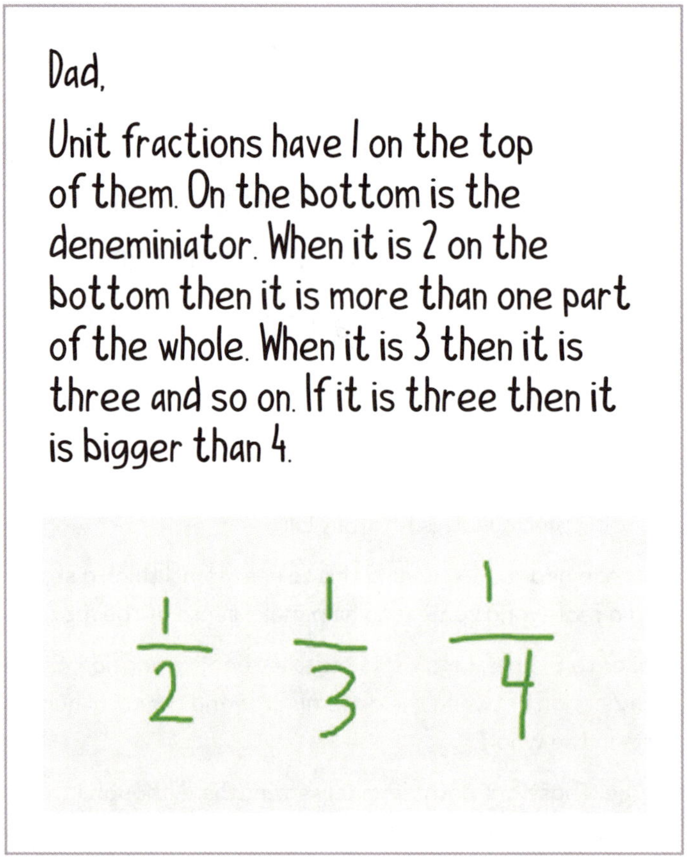

> Dad,
> Unit fractions have 1 on the top of them. On the bottom is the deneminiator. When it is 2 on the bottom then it is more than one part of the whole. When it is 3 then it is three and so on. If it is three then it is bigger than 4.
>
> $\frac{1}{2}$ $\frac{1}{3}$ $\frac{1}{4}$

78   Part 3   Asset-Based Conferring: How Does Focusing on Students' Strengths Support Them in Making Conjectures?

KARLA: I am really wanting him to explore with concrete manipulatives like Cuisenaire rods. I think the way to do that is to build off the strength of creating a visual. This appears to be an attempt to put the fractions in order. I think we could name that. It is useful for mathematicians to organize numbers in meaningful ways.

TINA: Yeah, I might ask him to tell me more about the order in which he has written the fractions. If that elicits information that confirms that he has attempted to put them in order, I might say, "Ordering the fractions from least to greatest is a really useful way to communicate and share your ideas about the sizes of the fractions. Creating this representation was an important decision that will help others to understand what you are trying to communicate about these numbers."

JAY: I like that. That would enable me to help Zeke to build on that strength by asking him to explore other representations to go along with this thinking. I might even suggest that he collaborate with Lili so that he can explore a more concrete visual that he might connect back to the pizza slices problems we've been working on.

MITCHELL: Absolutely. This would really help make the mathematics visible for him and may cause him to reconsider his initial thinking.

Naming Strengths Fosters Positive Math Identities

If you are like me, after a few conferences, you may worry that you selected the wrong strength, or worry that you didn't notice the right strength. Conferring is the type of process in which there are many right choices! Every skill and mathematical decision you name and reinforce will benefit your mathematicians. Each time you name a strength, you are validating your students' abilities and communicating to them and those around them that they are capable mathematicians. In turn, students will generally be more open to you as you nudge them forward in their learning. And if you're lucky you will start to notice a very specific type of smile after you name your students' strengths. Although they are sometimes small and almost shy-looking smiles, you won't want to miss them. These are the smiles of proud mathematicians.

Chapter 7

Nudging Student Thinking and Inviting Conjecture in *Beyond the Task* Conferences

Recently, I was thinking back to when I took my first high school geometry class. I remember learning the Pythagorean Theorem and feeling confident using $a^2 + b^2 = c^2$ to solve for *a*, *b*, or *c*. It never occurred to me that my confidence wasn't related to understanding the theorem but rather to my ability to plug numbers into the equation and get an answer.

As a high school student, why didn't it bother me that I didn't understand? Why didn't I ask more questions? Well, because I knew that Pythagoras had already figured it out. Why should I spend my time wondering? My identity was that of a high school math student and not a real mathematician. It never occurred to me that I should work like a mathematician in school. Later in life, when I stumbled upon a visual for this theorem (**Figure 7.1**), I felt a little disappointed. The visual made sense to me, and I found it interesting. I began to wonder how many more interesting math concepts I had missed.

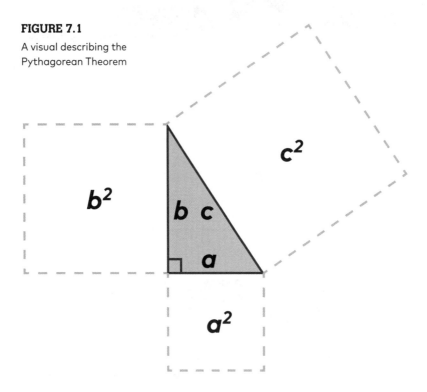

FIGURE 7.1

A visual describing the Pythagorean Theorem

Later, as an educator, I wanted my students to have a different experience learning mathematics starting in elementary school. I wanted them to know that there was more to math than following a set of procedures to get an answer. I wanted them to have space to ask questions, notice patterns, and come up with their own ideas about how and why something works. Most importantly, I wanted my students to be independent mathematicians who take an active role in their learning. So how do we get students to take on this kind of agency?

Nudging from What Was Named and Reinforced

Naming and reinforcing students' strengths is a powerful component of conferring because it is a public way that we can build students' confidence and develop their math identities. Once the decision has been made to confer *Beyond the Task*, an effective move is to ask students a question that nudges their thinking directly from the named strength (**Table 7.1**). This conferring move is effective for two reasons: (1) students' ideas and strengths drive the work, and (2) the structure of the conference becomes predictable for students and teachers.

TABLE 7.1

Questions to nudge students' thinking

Possible Questions that Nudge Students' Thinking *Beyond the Task*

Do you think this always works?
Would this work if _____?
When wouldn't this work?
Do you think this only works with _____?
When is this strategy useful?
Would this work with other types of numbers?
Would this work when using a different operation?

Students' Ideas Should Drive the Work

When conferring with writers, Calkins, Hartman, and White suggest "teaching into a child's intentions" (2005, 71). Specifically, they recommend guiding students toward the goals that they are already working on or interested in, rather than taking the writer down a different path. This focus ensures that the students are the decision makers and retain a sense of agency over their work. The same reasoning can be applied to math conferences. Nudging students in a direction that is not related to the strength that you just named might leave them wondering if the strength was truly important or useful after all.

Keeping the Conference Predictable

Nudging students from what was named and reinforced also keeps the conference structure predictable for students and teachers. From the student's perspective, after you have named something they have done that is useful or interesting as a mathematician, they can expect that you will either invite them to share their ideas with others in the math community (*Within the Task*) or nudge them toward considering the idea outside of the task and make a conjecture (*Beyond the Task*). Unpredictable conferences may cause students to focus their attention on trying to figure out what the conference is about rather than focusing on the mathematics. Carl Anderson shares a similar belief about conferring with readers and writers: "When I have watched teachers who are good at conferring, I've noticed that their conversations with students are shaped by a structure. Because these teachers know in general how they want their conversations with students to go—as do their students, once they've been in several conferences—the talk flows easily and naturally, and both the teachers and students hold up their end of the talk" (2000, 16). This natural and predictable flow is an important part of math conferences. After multiple conferring experiences, you might even notice some students making generalizations and conjectures without being nudged.

Inviting Students to Make Conjectures

Making conjectures can sound a little intimidating. You might be wondering if this is something young mathematicians can really do. They surely can! This is work our students are already doing and do quite naturally. It is human nature to observe patterns and to use those patterns to develop ideas about when and how things work. For example, when my son was about five years old, we took a family trip to a local Texas beach. Being an Austinite, he had plenty of experience swimming in lakes but not as much familiarity with oceans. On the trip he made a big observation: the water in the ocean tasted salty and the water in the lake didn't. He followed this up with two big questions: "Are all oceans salty?" and "Where did the salt come from?" I replied to his wonderings with, "Great questions! What do you think?" He paused for a few seconds and said, "I think the rocks must have salt on them and the waves are breaking the rocks and putting salt into the ocean." His interest in making observations about the world around him and then trying to make sense of and generalize these observations was natural. As teachers, we can tap into our students' natural curiosity and help them to take the patterns that they notice and develop them into conjectures.

So, what exactly are conjectures? They are statements that mathematicians believe to be true but have not yet proven or explored fully. In the words of Marian Small, author of *Understanding the Math We Teach and How to Teach It*, "A conjecture is a conclusion or opinion that has not yet been verified that students might wonder about" (2019, 28). To develop a conjecture, a mathematician needs a preliminary hypothesis which the students develop as they are investigating their ideas. These conjectures, along with the evidence, become public so that other mathematicians can consider them and attempt to prove or disprove them. With time and space for this important work, every student can develop conjectures to share with the math community. Let's take a look at the chart in **Table 7.2** for a few examples of students' conjectures at different grade levels.

TABLE 7.2

Examples of Student-Made Conjectures

Grade Level	Conjecture
Kindergarten	Counting by tens takes less time than counting by ones.
First Grade	Any two numbers can be added in any order, and you will get the same sum.
Second Grade	If the unit of measurement is small, it will take more units to measure an object than if you use larger units.
Third Grade	If two fractions have the same denominator, each of the wholes was partitioned into the same number of pieces.
Fourth Grade	A triangle can have no more than one right angle.
Fifth Grade	The product of a decimal that is less than one and a whole number will always be less than the whole number.

Let's take a closer look at nudging and inviting students to make conjectures by visiting Mark Uhler's fifth-grade classroom and Elysha Dante's kindergarten classroom. Although the students in these classrooms are working on different mathematics concepts and at different grade levels, each teacher follows the same *Beyond the Task* conferring structure. As you read, notice how each teacher transitions from nudging students to extending an invitation to make conjectures.

A *Beyond the Task* Conference with Fifth Grader Jasmine

After presenting a math task involving fractions to his fifth graders, Mark walks around his classroom to observe his students as they get started. He notices that Jasmine is seated at a circular table with two of her classmates. After taking a closer look he sees that the two students at the table are working together and that Jasmine is quietly but quickly writing something in her notebook. Mark approaches the table and decides to confer with Jasmine first. As he confers with her, he is hoping to find an opportunity to encourage Jasmine to work collaboratively with the other mathematicians. Mark has noticed that sometimes Jasmine chooses to work alone but with a little encouragement, she will usually share her thinking with others. Mark also knows that, as a mathematician, Jasmine often comes up with creative strategies, and he hopes that encouraging Jasmine to share her ideas with the math community will not only have a positive effect on Jasmine's math identity but will also prompt other students to take creative risks too.

MARK: Hi, Jasmine! What are you working on?

JASMINE: I knew I had to multiply, so I changed the fraction to be easier to multiply.

MARK: Tell me more about this. It looks interesting!

JASMINE: I saw the $5/8$ and changed it to $4/8$ or $1/2$ and $1/8$.

MARK: Tell me more. I see that $1/2$ plus $1/8$ is $5/8$, but why did you do that?

JASMINE: It is just something I do. I can figure out half of 6. So, I took the $1/2$ out of the $5/8$. Then I knew $1/2 \times 6$ was three. All I had to do then was figure out $1/8 \times 6$ and add it to the 3.

MARK: Wow. So, you decomposed $5/8$ into two addends: $4/8$ and $1/8$. Then you used the distributive property and multiplied 6 by each of those addends?

JASMINE: Yeah.

MARK: Being flexible with numbers in order to work with them more easily is really useful! Do you think this strategy works all the time?

JASMINE: I don't know. Probably.

MARK: I am wondering if this strategy only works when the fraction you want to decompose is greater than $1/2$. Can you always break a fraction down into smaller parts and multiply them separately?

JASMINE: I think so. . . . Yeah, it should work, right?

MARK: I wonder if you can do some work to try to figure out when this works. If you figure it out, I think our math community would love to hear your conjecture. I think your classmates will find this strategy interesting and might want to try it out. By the way, a couple of days ago, I saw Ricardo using the distributive property with whole numbers. You might ask him if he would like to collaborate with you in this work.

In this conference, Mark nudged Jasmine to think about how this strategy would work with different numbers. Asking students to consider when something works and when it doesn't work encourages them to think critically about mathematical processes or properties, in this case how the distributive property works with fractions less than one half. This encouragement and nudge to think deeply about their work gives students the time and space to discover bigger mathematical ideas and gain a deeper understanding of the strategies and procedures that they are using.

Fifth Graders Ricardo and Jasmine Gather Evidence for Their Conjecture

Gathering evidence is the work that students engage in after the teacher has walked away from a *Beyond the Task* conference. Let's listen in on Ricardo and Jasmine's conversation as they make a plan for their work together:

JASMINE: Hi, Ricardo. Mr. Uhler said that we could maybe work on a conjecture together.

RICARDO: What is it about?

JASMINE: Well, when I was working on the task I broke ⅝ down into 4/8 and ⅛. [*shows Ricardo her work* (**Figure 7.2**)] Mr. Uhler said sometimes you do something similar. Then he was asking if it would work if the fraction is less than ½.

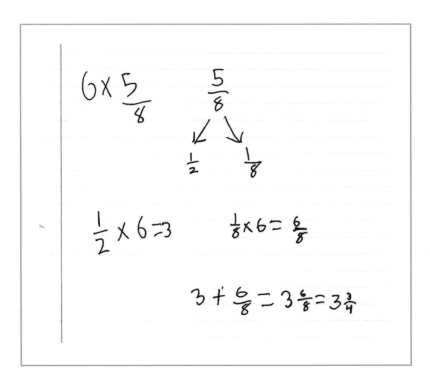

FIGURE 7.2 Jasmine's work solving 6 × ⅝

RICARDO: What do you mean?

JASMINE: Well, like if the fraction that I decompose is less than ½, could I still break it into two parts and multiply them separately?

RICARDO: I think you can.

JASMINE: Me too. Do you want to work together?

RICARDO: Sure.

JASMINE: So, let's make some problems with a whole number and fraction smaller than ½ that we can multiply together.

RICARDO: Okay, how about 4 and ⅓. Okay. I will write [**Figure 7.3**]. So, we can break ⅓ into ⅙ and ⅙.

JASMINE: Yeah, then you'd get 4/6 + 4/6 after you multiply by four.

RICARDO: Cool. We get 8/6.

JASMINE: Maybe we should simplify it.

RICARDO: Okay 1 and 2/6. Actually 1 and ⅓.

JASMINE: Let's do another one.

RICARDO: Maybe we should solve this one another way first to show that we actually got the correct answer.

JASMINE: Yeah. Just put 4/3, because four one-thirds is 4/3.

RICARDO: Done. 4/3 is equal to 1 and ⅓.

JASMINE: Should we also do one where the fraction is more than one half? That would show that it works with fractions larger than ½ too.

RICARDO: Okay, like what?

JASMINE: Maybe 5 × ⅗. Plus when we share with the class, I can show my work from the original problem too.

RICARDO: Okay. We can change ⅗ to 3/10 and 3/10.

JASMINE: Yeah then you'd get 15/10 plus 15/10.

RICARDO: 30/10, which is 3.

JASMINE: Then we can just multiply across for the second strategy and get 15/5, which is also 3.

Chapter 7 Nudging Student Thinking and Inviting Conjecture in *Beyond the Task* Conferences

FIGURE 7.3

The evidence that Jasmine and Ricardo developed to share with the math community

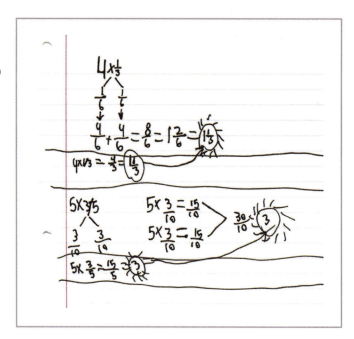

Fifth Graders Jasmine and Ricardo Revise Their Conjecture and Attend to Precision

Now that Jasmine and Ricardo have developed an idea and have some preliminary evidence to support the idea, they are ready to create the first draft of their conjecture. When supporting students with this drafting work, it is helpful to remind them that, like all drafts, their first attempt at a conjecture will often need revisions. Because students will share their conjectures with the math community, they will likely feel motivated to make sure that they are written in a way that others can understand.

To support students as they make revisions, you might consider posting an anchor chart in the classroom that lists possible steps for the revision process (**Figures 7.4** and **7.5**). Students can review the anchor chart to ensure that they have followed all the steps before presenting their work. A word wall or pocket chart with math vocabulary is also helpful so that students can refer to it and revise for precise vocabulary (**Figure 7.6**).

FIGURE 7.4

Example of a revising checklist used in a fifth-grade classroom

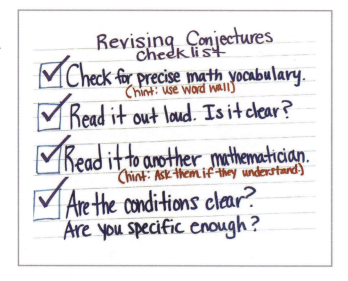

88 Part 3 Asset-Based Conferring: How Does Focusing on Students' Strengths Support Them in Making Conjectures?

FIGURE 7.5

Example of a sharing conjectures anchor chart used in a kindergarten classroom

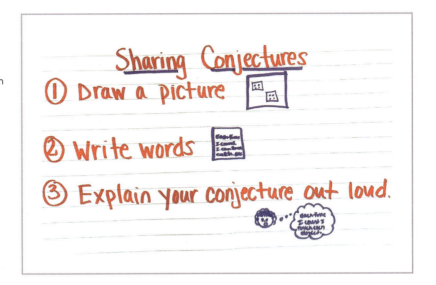

FIGURE 7.6

Math vocabulary displayed in a pocket chart in a kindergarten classroom. The blue sticky notes show language the class added as they began to use increasingly precise language

After some experience creating and presenting conjectures, students will come to realize that the revision process is important. Their ideas matter and they will want to make sure that they communicate them in ways that are clear and understandable to their classmates. Let's take a look at Jasmine and Ricardo's rough and revised drafts of their conjecture (**Figures 7.7** and **7.8**).

Chapter 7   Nudging Student Thinking and Inviting Conjecture in *Beyond the Task* Conferences   **89**

FIGURE 7.7

Jasmine and Ricardo's first and second drafts of their conjecture

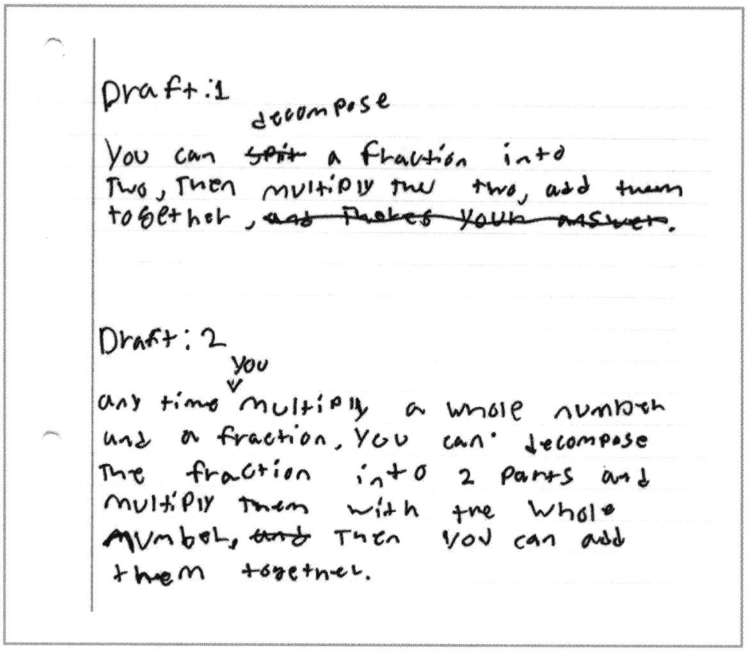

> Draft: 1
>
> decompose
> You can ~~split~~ a fraction into two, then multiply the two, add them together, ~~and~~ ~~thats~~ ~~your~~ ~~answer~~.
>
> Draft: 2
>
> you
> any time ^ multiply a whole number and a fraction, you can decompose the fraction into 2 parts and multiply them with the whole number, ~~and~~ Then you can add them together.

FIGURE 7.8

Jasmine and Ricardo's final conjecture

> Anytime you multiply a whole number and a fraction, you can decompose the fraction into two parts and multiply them with the whole number. Then you can add them together.

Now Jasmine and Ricardo are ready to share their work with the math community. Although the distributive property of multiplication is not a new discovery for all mathematicians, considering how this property works for rational numbers is a new and important concept for the fifth-grade students in this classroom. Jasmine and Ricardo's understanding of how this property works with rational numbers was deepened as they collaborated and reasoned together. Additionally, the classroom math community will benefit from having an opportunity to consider this conjecture and agree or disagree with it. Before we listen in on Jasmine and Ricardo as they share their conjecture with their classmates, let's visit Elysha Dante's classroom and see how this conjecture process could look with kindergarten students.

A *Beyond the Task* Conference with Kindergarteners Davis and Jonah

As Elysha walks around her classroom, she notices two of her students, Davis and Jonah, sitting together on the carpet with a large box of multi-colored teddy bear counters. They have taken several of them out and placed them into one long line. There are several number sense and counting principles that Elysha hopes to see her kindergarteners develop this year. As she approaches Davis and Jonah, she wonders if she might see evidence of subitizing to five (instantly recognizing how many without counting), cardinality (knowing that the last number said when counting represents the total amount in the set), one-to-one correspondence (counting each object once and only once), or other strategies that support counting.

FIGURE 7.9
Davis touches the teddy bear counters as he counts out loud

ELYSHA: Wow, you have so many teddy bears here. What are you doing?

DAVIS: Counting.

ELYSHA: Davis, after watching you, I noticed you did something interesting. Can I ask you about it?

DAVIS: Yeah.

ELYSHA: As you counted, you touched each teddy bear (**Figure 7.9**). Why did you do that?

DAVIS: I like to.

JONAH: I do that too. Watch. [*touches each bear as he counts*]

ELYSHA: Why do you like to do that?

JONAH: Sometimes I count and do it like this. [*demonstrates counting fast and counting some teddy bears more than once*]

ELYSHA: Oh! So, when you touch each one, that doesn't happen?

DAVIS: No, because we touch it when we count it.

ELYSHA: I see. What a great idea. You touch each bear to make sure you count each one only once. That seems to be helpful. Do you think this is something mathematicians should do all the time or just sometimes?

Chapter 7 Nudging Student Thinking and Inviting Conjecture in *Beyond the Task* Conferences

DAVIS: Every time.

ELYSHA: Is there a time when a mathematician would not need to do that?

JONAH: If they just have one. [*laughing*]

ELYSHA: Hmm. I think you two have discovered something. Counting objects only once is important. You have found that touching each object helps you to keep track of your counting. You also have ideas about when mathematicians need to use this strategy. Can you grab one of the small posters and start to work on a conjecture? Remember, you can write the sentences if you can, or you can draw a picture and explain it when you share it with the class. Do you think you can start to work on that now? Our math community will be excited to hear about this.

FIGURE 7.10

Davis and Jonah's conjecture

"Mathematicians can touch each one when there are a lot."

In this conference, Elysha was excited to see Davis touching each teddy bear as he counted. She was equally excited to hear Jonah announce that he does this too! As a kindergarten teacher, she knows that one-to-one correspondence and tagging is an important and useful idea and strategy for young mathematicians. In addition, Elysha thought that some students in her class might begin to use this strategy if they heard about it from Davis and Jonah. Elysha was purposeful in inviting Davis and Jonah to record the sentence only if they could (**Figure 7.10**). It is important to ensure that our youngest mathematicians do not see writing ability as a barrier to sharing their conjectures.

Kindergarteners Davis and Jonah, and fifth graders Jasmine and Ricardo, demonstrated that they were capable of thinking about and developing conjectures in response to the nudge their teachers gave them during their conferences. In many ways, conferring is a way of giving our students an invitation to join the math community and share their ideas and knowledge. With strong conferring practices in place and a collaborative classroom environment, students will often start to respond to the predictable nature of the conference by engaging in this work without an invitation. They will understand that their teacher is there to support them, but that their direction and ideas are all their own!

Guiding Students to Share Their Conjectures During the Community Share

Setting up expectations for the community share is an important part of ensuring that students feel comfortable and confident explaining their conjectures as well as responding to the ideas of their peers. Reviewing the expectations at the start of each community share is a great way to keep this part of the math block predictable for students, so that they can focus on expressing their ideas and listening to their fellow mathematicians. Prior to inviting Jasmine and Ricardo up to the front of the room to share their conjecture, fifth-grade teacher Mark Uhler displayed his Community Share Expectations slides for his class to review (**Figure 7.11**).

FIGURE 7.11

Community share expectations slides for Mark Uhler's fifth-grade classroom

Community Share Expectations for the Presenting Mathematicians

- Share your conjecture under the document camera.
- Read the conjecture slowly and clearly.
- Present evidence under the document camera.
- Ask the math community for their questions, arguments, or suggestions.
- Decide to revise the conjecture or post it for public use.

Community Share Expectations for the Audience

- Look at the presenting mathematicians and their work.
- Ask clarifying questions such as, "I don't understand _____. Can you explain _____ again?"
- Make statements of agreement such as, "I agree with _____ because _____."
- Make statement of disagreement such as, "I disagree with _____ because _____."
- Make suggestions such as, "I wonder if you could try _____."

Let's see how Mark facilitated the community share in his fifth-grade classroom.

MARK: Alright everyone. I know some of you are in the middle of your work, but we need to break away and join together for the community share. We have a few mathematicians ready to share their ideas. Nice job getting to the carpet quickly, mathematicians. Let's review our expectations. [*calls on two students to read the expectations to the class*] During our last share, I noticed we all did a great job listening to our presenters, but we didn't have much feedback to offer. Remember we made the decision that today we would try turning and talking to one another to see if that helps us give clear and specific feedback. Let's have Ricardo and Jasmine come up and present their conjecture first.

RICARDO: Jasmine and I came up with this conjecture after working on the problem. [*Jasmine places the conjecture under the document camera (**Figure 7.8**)*]. Anytime you multiply a whole number and a fraction, you can decompose the fraction into two parts, and multiply them with the whole number. Then you can add them together.

JASMINE: We tried this out with a few problems. Actually, at first, I did this when I was solving by myself. [*places her original work under the document camera (**Figure 7.2**)*] I decomposed $5/8$ into $4/8$ and $1/8$. I did this because $4/8$ is a half and that would be easier for me to think about. I know that $1/2$ of six is three. So that part was done.

RICARDO: So then we came up with more evidence.

MARK: Before you move on, this might be a good time to ask your fellow mathematicians if they understand your thinking.

RICARDO: Do you have questions?

MARK: Why don't we turn and talk and see what questions we can come up with. [*The students turn and talk to those sitting next to them on the carpet.*] What questions do you have?

KYLA: We don't understand what you mean when you say half of six. Why did you take half of six?

JASMINE: Because finding one half times a number is easy for me because you can just take half of the number. So one half times six is three.

RICARDO: Yeah, you can make the calculation that it is $6/2$, which is three.

MARK: Great question, Kyla and Jenny. I overheard your conversation about this. This might be something that the two of you could investigate further. We all might benefit from exploring the different ways to think about multiplying rational numbers.

KYLA: Yeah, I think I get it. I agree that it is three. That's just not how I did it.

RICARDO: So then we did two more problems [*pointing to their work under the document camera (**Figure 7.3**)*]. Both times we decomposed the fractions into two parts. We multiplied them separately and then added them.

JASMINE: We did them two ways to prove that we would get the same answer [*reading the work from the evidence she and Ricardo developed*].

MARK: Let's turn and talk and see if you can come up with questions, suggestions, or feedback for Ricardo and Jasmine. Let's review some of the examples of how to word that feedback [*displays his second expectations slide on the classroom projector* (**Figure 7.11**)].

REECE: I agree with Ricardo and Jasmine that you can break a fraction into parts and multiply the parts separately. Derrick and I don't think it is always useful. Like the last example of five times $^3/_5$. It is just easier to do $^{15}/_5$, which is 3. I don't think that strategy is the best strategy for that problem.

JASMINE: I agree, but we were just trying to prove that it would work. But yeah, I don't think $^3/_{10}$ was any easier to work with than $^3/_5$.

MARK: Reece and Derrick, tell us more about your thinking. Were there any problems that you thought were strong examples of when you might want to use this strategy?

DERRICK: Yeah. When Jasmine did it with the original problem. It made sense because she was able to multiply six by one half.

JASMINE: I agree. I think when the fraction has one half in it, then the strategy makes solving easier.

MARK: Does anyone have any other thoughts or some possible counterexamples?

ALEXIS: I agree that this strategy works. Kayla and I talked about how we do this with whole numbers sometimes during number talks [*a mental math routine that the class engages during the fluency portion of the math block*]. So it is really the same thing.

MARK: Tell me more about how this connects to the work you do during number talks.

ALEXIS: Well, like last week we did a problem that was 5 x 38 or something like that. A lot of us said we multiplied 5 x 30 and then 5 x 8. That's kind of the same thing.

MARK: I see. So this strategy, which uses the distributive property, works similarly when both factors are whole numbers. Jasmine and Ricardo, do you feel you need to take this back and make any revisions based on the feedback from the community, or do you want to post it publicly?

RICARDO: We can post it. [*hands the conjecture and evidence to Mark to display on the classroom wall*]

MARK: As always, this will be displayed on the wall so that anyone in the math community can try it out. If you find counterexamples, it will be important to bring those back to the community for discussion.

The community share portion of the math block is a key ingredient for successful conferences because the opportunity to share ideas publicly shifts the audience from the teacher to the classroom math community. With this shift in audience, students understand that the purpose of developing a conjecture or sharing a strategy is to add to the collective mathematical understanding of their community. In Mark's classroom, the students know that their teacher will facilitate the community share by encouraging students to ask questions and provide feedback, but their focus is not on Mark during this time. Mark treats his students as the lead decision makers and positions their ideas as important and useful. In fact, their ideas are so important and useful that he displays them on the walls to be revisited throughout the year.

Chapter 7   Nudging Student Thinking and Inviting Conjecture in *Beyond the Task* Conferences

Part 4

Planning for Success:

What Should You Consider Before Conferring?

Chapter 8

Building a Math Community that Fosters Positive Math Identities

One evening a few years ago I got an email from Loretta Bearden, a fourth-grade teacher, telling me how excited she was about a symmetry lesson that she had just planned. She had created a task that she hoped would increase student discourse, and she wanted to know if I could watch the lesson and give her feedback. I am so glad that I was able to visit her class that day; what I saw made me wish I could visit her math class every day! The task she developed was purposeful and effective, but what really caught my attention was the way her class felt like a collaborative math community from the moment the lesson began.

During math conferences, we communicate to students that they are one member of a math community with significant ideas to contribute. But what about the rest of the math block? It is so important that the positive community we encourage during conferences doesn't only exist within a conference. Loretta's classroom was a great example of how that sense of community can be fostered throughout the math block.

Fourth-Grade Symmetry Lesson

As I stepped into Loretta's classroom, I could hear the morning announcements playing through the monitor in the front of the room. Once the announcements were over, Loretta called the kids to the carpet. I expected her to say something like, "Come to the carpet. It is time for math." But instead, she gave the students a much more exciting invitation:

LORETTA: Good morning, everyone! As you finish up making your lunch choice, please join me at the carpet. Something really interesting happened to me after school yesterday. Actually, I am feeling really weird about what happened. So I decided to make it into a math task, because I really want you to help me out with it. [*students start walking to the carpet*]

CORINNA: What happened, Mrs. Bearden?

LORETTA: So, Mrs. Deale and I were planning the math task for today. We were going to explore cut-outs of capital letters and find the lines of symmetry. I was trying to make a chart to help us organize the information. I said that we would need to make a place to record the nine letters that have zero lines of symmetry. Mrs. Deale said that there are actually ten letters that have no lines of symmetry. I really think I am right, but I want to be sure. I was thinking that you all could help me with this today. [*displays the task* (**Figure 8.1**)]

FIGURE 8.1

Symmetry math task

> Mrs. Deale says that 10 capital letters have no lines of symmetry. Mrs. Bearden says that 9 capital letters have no lines of symmetry.
>
> Who do you agree with and why?

LORETTA: What is this task about? Turn and talk to the mathematician sitting next to you. [*students turn and talk*] Who would like to share what you and your partner talked about?

CHASE: You and Mrs. Deale don't agree. You think nine letters have no lines of symmetry and she thinks ten of them don't.

LORETTA: What tools might be useful for your work today?

PRISHA: We might need some shapes or maybe we could draw them.

LORETTA: Great idea. I have a set of paper capital letters for each group. You are free to use them in any way that you want. I won't be reusing them, so don't worry about trying to keep them nice. What else?

JAXON: Did you make a chart for us to record on?

LORETTA: No, I didn't end up making one. Maybe as a group, you can come up with a way to record and keep track of the information.

PRISHA: So if we can cut them, maybe scissors would be good.

LORETTA: Oh, good thinking. I think we are off to a great start. If there are other tools that you need and can't find them, let me know. One more thing. Are there any words on our vocabulary wall that might help us to be precise and clear when we are working on this task?

JAXON: Symmetry. [*laughing*]

LORETTA: Yes, we will definitely be using that word. Any others?

TAYLOR: Horizontal, vertical, and diagonal.

LORETTA: Those seem useful too! Okay, before you work with your groups, take a few minutes to work on this independently first. At your seats, I would like you to brainstorm ways to approach this task and draft out a table that could help you keep track of the work [**Figure 8.2**].

FIGURE 8.2
Independent portion of the task

Independent Work Time

How might you start this work? How might you keep track of the work?

LORETTA: [*after independent work time*] Okay, it is time to begin working with your group. Be sure to share your ideas with the group. One person from each group can collect the tools that you want to use and pick up a baggie with the letters.

Students quickly got up from their seats, gathered supplies, and began working with their groups. The room was buzzing with action as students shared their ideas for how to start this work and how to organize the information. Sadly, I had to leave before the community share because I was meeting another teacher. I couldn't wait to meet with Loretta that afternoon. I would certainly give her feedback on the task, as she had requested, but what I couldn't wait to talk about was how she had developed such a positive and collaborative math community.

Meeting with Loretta

When I approached Loretta's room, I noticed that she wasn't back from bus duty yet. As I stood outside her classroom door, I started thinking about what it means to have a strong math community. What was it about her classroom that felt like a community of mathematicians rather than a classroom of individual students working on a math problem? I made a mental list of the things that I noticed.

1. The students seemed genuinely interested in the task.
2. The students did a lot of talking and sharing of ideas.
3. The students seemed to know the structure and flow of the math block.
4. The students seemed eager to get to work.
5. The students were leading the work.

A few minutes later, Loretta came walking down the hall. She seemed just as eager as I was to talk about the lesson.

LORETTA: Hi! So what did you think?

GINA: I loved it! I am so bummed I had to miss the community share.

LORETTA: Oh, I wish you could have seen it too. They were so into the task. They came up with some great ways to check for lines of symmetry and they seemed to really enjoy proving me wrong. [*laughing*]

GINA: You and Mrs. Deale disagreeing about lines of symmetry was such a great idea for a math task. Not only was it interesting, but it provided an opportunity for so much discourse between students. That is one of the things I noticed even as you were introducing the task. You gave the kids time to talk about the task before working on it, which made it more accessible. The other thing that I noticed was that you have developed a strong community of mathematicians. They seemed to take so much ownership in the work and seemed experienced at sharing ideas with one another. Is this something you work on or something that just happened naturally?

LORETTA: I work on this a lot! At my old school, we learned a lot about forming a classroom community. I took some of those ideas and some other things that I have learned over the years about math communities and tried to put those things in place.

GINA: What types of things?

LORETTA: The way I structure the time during the math block, using tasks that can be solved in more than one way, and forming student groups that are not related to ability. These are all things that I have developed over the years. We also spend time throughout the year talking about how to share ideas and how to disagree. But those three things are kind of the glue that holds it all together. My students know what to expect each day. I do too, which I really like!

Loretta suggested three things that she feels are helpful for developing a community of collaborative mathematicians. Let's consider each of those suggestions, how they looked in Loretta's classroom, and how they support the development of community and positive math identities (**Table 8.1**).

TABLE 8.1

Suggestions for Building a Collaborative Community

Suggestions	What This Looked Like in Loretta's Classroom	How It Builds a Sense of Community and Positive Math Identities
Following a predictable sequence of math activities during the math block	A math block structured in this way: • Task introduction • Independent work time • Group work time • Community share	A predictable sequence of activities helps students to keep their full attention on the mathematics and the sharing of ideas. This structure helps students feel a sense of agency and control over their work.
Using open middle math tasks	Tasks in which there are more than one method students can use to solve.	These types of tasks give students opportunities to share different ideas and see multiple ways of solving. These tasks help students to see value in their own ideas and the ideas of their peers.
Forming mixed-ability groups	Students work in groups that change throughout the year and are not based on ability.	This way of grouping communicates to students that they are all valued members of a math community. This type of grouping provides opportunities for all students to learn from one another and see themselves and their peers as capable mathematicians.

There are many ways to structure the math block, math tasks, and student groups. The most important things to consider when making these decisions is how it will impact students' ideas about the purpose of mathematics and their roles and abilities as mathematicians. Students' math identities are shaped by every experience they have with mathematics. Each instructional decision we make can intentionally or unintentionally affect students' beliefs about themselves as mathematicians and what they believe about their peers. The healthiest math communities are ones where every student feels a sense of belonging and understands that when they share ideas, the whole community benefits.

Chapter 9

Planning for Data Collection and Analysis

When I was in third grade, I was placed into the Diplodocus math group. Although my teacher never told us that our math groups were based on our abilities, I was sure that this slow-moving dinosaur symbolized my mathematical understanding. Luckily, my feelings about myself as a mathematician improved in later years, but even now I wonder how my group placement was decided. What data could have shown that I was an overall poor math student? Why did my teacher think I would benefit from only working with other students that were also perceived as having low abilities in math? I may never know what type of data guided my teacher's decision, but I know that being placed in the Diplodocus math group had a negative impact on my math identity.

Gathering data from math conferences is a great way to make instructional decisions that target students' needs, but our students' math identities should always be at the forefront of our minds as we interpret data. Before we explore how to gather data from math conferences, let's consider what conferring data can and cannot show us (**Table 9.1**).

TABLE 9.1

What Conferring Data Can and Cannot Show Us

	What Conferring Data Can Show Us	What Conferring Data Cannot Show Us
Individual Students	• The concepts students have been nudged to explore • The concepts and ideas that students are grappling with • Students' strengths that have been named and reinforced • The types of conferences (*Within the Task* or *Beyond the Task*) students have had and when	• Students' ability levels
Group of Students	• Which students are grappling with similar ideas and concepts	• Which students have the same mathematical abilities
Whole Class	• The concepts and ideas the majority of the class is grappling with • How often a conference cycle is completed	• How one class compares academically to another class

Gathering Data During Conferences

Several years ago, while I was in my second year teaching kindergarten, my principal asked if I would be open to letting other teachers observe how I collect data during the math block. I remember that his request made me feel uneasy. My principal seemed impressed that I was collecting data, but my secret was that I didn't really do much with the data. My clipboard used to get so filled with notes that I would take the papers, file them in the cabinet, replace my clipboard with fresh paper, and start over. I learned a great deal from my students by kneeling down beside them and conferring, but the amount of notes I was taking was a little overwhelming to make sense of. In fact, the papers rarely came back out of the filing cabinet.

In the years since this teaching experience, I have come to realize that data collection doesn't need to fill filing cabinets in order to be useful. In fact, I have found the opposite to be true. Collecting just a few key pieces of data during a conference gives me the information I need to make specific and intentional instructional decisions for individual students, groups of students, and the whole class. Let's take a look at the collections of data that two teachers gathered while conferring with first-grade and fifth-grade students (**Figures 9.1** and **9.2**). In both examples, the teachers used a conferring notes template (**Appendix C**) to record the strengths they named and reinforced during the conferences, the concepts or ideas that they nudged, and the types of conferences they used.

FIGURE 9.1

First-grade conferring notes

Math Conferring Data Week of 9/12
Unit: First Grade/Representing Data

Chad and Ling	Talla, Ayaka, and Minyoung	Tyrell and Neil	Jessie and Sun-Hee
Named and Reinforced: Represented the data with connecting cubes and tally marks	**Named and Reinforced:** Represented data by showing the sum of two categories using an addition equation	**Named and Reinforced:** Organized data into towers of connecting cubes and made statements comparing the number in each category	**Named and Reinforced:** Drew dots to represent the data and labeled each category to show what the dots represent
Nudged to: Consider and share similarities and differences between these representations.	**Nudged to:** Investigate how addition equations can be used to represent other data sets, including sets with more than two categories.	**Nudged to:** Consider and share how organizing connecting cubes helped them interpret the data.	**Nudged to:** Investigate the types of information that can be included in data representations to help others understand the data.
(Within Task) / Beyond Task	Within Task / (Beyond Task) Shared conjecture 9/12	(Within Task) / Beyond Task	Within Task / (Beyond Task) Shared conjecture 9/13

Chapter 9   Planning for Data Collection and Analysis   **107**

FIGURE 9.2
Fifth-grade conferring notes

Math Conferring Data Week of 10/5
Unit: Fifth Grade/Decimal Multiplication

Janelle, Aria, and Li	Farrah and Leila	Daysha and Trent	Cho and Imani
Named and Reinforced: Rounded and estimated the product before solving. Janelle: "1.08 × 15 is about 15, because 1.08 is close to 1 and 1 × 15 is 15."	**Named and Reinforced:** Solved 1.5 × 8 using the distributive property: (1 × 8) + (.5 × 8).	**Named and Reinforced:** Reasoned about the size of the product before solving .48 × 20. Trent: "This means forty-eight hundredths of 20. So the product has to be less than 20. And .48 is less than half. So the answer has to be less than 10."	**Named and Reinforced:** Creating an equivalent fraction to find the product of 1.5 × 8. Cho: "1.5 is 1½. I can add 1½ eight times. One 8 times is 8 and ½ eight times is 4."
Nudged to: Investigate how rounding might work when both factors are decimals	**Nudged to:** Investigate how the distributive property works when both factors are decimals	**Nudged to:** Consider and share more than one way to reason about the product of .48 and 20	**Nudged to:** Consider and share how this strategy was useful with this particular problem
Within Task **(Beyond Task)** Shared conjecture 10/5	Within Task **(Beyond Task)** Shared conjecture 10/6	**(Within Task)** Beyond Task	**(Within Task)** Beyond Task

108 Part 4 Planning for Success: What Should You Consider Before Conferring?

Analyzing the Data to Identify Trends

After my experience collecting and not using conferring data in kindergarten, I started trying out different ways to analyze the data. I wanted to structure this work in a way that didn't feel overwhelming. Conferring data can yield a lot of important information about individual students, groups of students, and the whole class, but I realized that it was too much information for me to digest at one time. To keep data analysis manageable, I find that it is helpful to decide ahead of time if I will be analyzing the data to inform whole-class instruction or small-group and individualized instruction. Recently, I met with a second-grade teacher named Vicky who was interested in analyzing her conferring data to inform whole-group instruction. Specifically, she wanted to use the data to help create math tasks for the following week that would target her students' needs. Let's listen in to find out what trends Vicky noticed in the conferring data, and how she used that information to plan math tasks for the following week.

Analyzing Second-Grade Conferring Data to Inform Whole-Class Instruction

VICKY: Hi, Gina. Thank you for meeting with me. I've been conferring with my students and have some data that I want to use to make math tasks for next week.

GINA: Yay! That is so exciting. How has conferring been going?

VICKY: I love it. I feel like I know my students better this year than I ever have, and it's only October!

GINA: That's amazing. I am so glad to hear that. So, you are just starting your measurement unit. Is that right?

VICKY: Yes, we started Tuesday and kicked it off with a really fun activity where the kids measured the backs of their chairs with paper clips. I didn't tell them that some groups were given large paperclips and some were given small ones. After they measured, they shared their measurements with other groups. The goal of this task is to help kids think about what they learned in first grade—about how to measure an object from end to end with no gaps—and then also for them to reason that we will get different measurements if we are using different sizes of units. That task lasted two days, and then on Thursday and Friday I gave them two other tasks where they used centimeter cubes to compare the lengths of objects in the room.

GINA: After conferring this week, what did you notice or wonder about your students' thinking?

VICKY: It seems like this unit is off to a good start. My students seem to understand the need for standard units, and many were measuring accurately by measuring from end to end without gaps between the units. There are a few students that I think need more practice and sometimes don't seem to notice when they haven't measured an object from end to end.

GINA: I am happy to hear it's going well. I'm excited to dig into the data and see what we can learn.

VICKY: So, how should we start?

GINA: Since our purpose today is to analyze the data to inform task creation, we can start by looking for trends in what you named and reinforced and what you nudged. When we are planning math tasks, we can notice the trends that extend beyond just a few students. A good general guideline is to interpret the data to notice what half or more of the students need.

VICKY: Many students noticed that using different sizes of paperclips resulted in different measurements. I nudged a few groups to consider how the size of the unit and the number of units needed to measure the object were related. I nudged them in this direction because that is the big idea in the math standard. I wonder if the class would benefit from exploring this concept again but in a different context.

GINA: I love that you are already using the trends to think about what students might need. Let's take another look at your data and record the strengths and nudges that appear the most in your conferring notes [**Figure 9.3**]. Then, beside each of those trends, jot down your thoughts about what your student might need.

FIGURE 9.3
Trends that Vicky noticed in the second-grade data

Vicky's Notes

Trends	Thoughts about What Students Need
Named and Reinforced: Most students explained that the size of the paperclip affected how many units were needed to measure the chair.	To generalize the inverse relationship between the number of units you need to measure an object and the size of the units you are using, they might need to explore units other than paperclips.
Nudged: Most students are still grappling with describing the inverse relationship between the number of units needed to measure an object and the size of the units.	They might benefit from opportunities to discover this inverse relationship by observing it as a pattern when measuring.

Part 4 Planning for Success: What Should You Consider Before Conferring?

Using Data to Inform Math Task Creation

Now that Vicky has taken notes on the trends and her thoughts about what students might need, it is time to use that information to inform what types of tasks will best meet her students' needs. Vicky believes that, based on the trends, her students need opportunities to engage in tasks that encourage them to use units other than paper clips and enable them to notice measurement patterns. Let's explore a few other whole-class needs that you might uncover from your data and how you might use that information to design future math tasks (**Table 9.2**).

TABLE 9.2

Using Data to Choose the Next Math Task

If you think your class would benefit from...	You might create a task that...	So that...
more exposure to the concept within the same context	is very similar to a previous task	students can focus on deepening their conceptual understanding rather than attending to a new context or problem type.
using more efficient strategies	encourages a particular strategy or strategies	students can discuss and compare this strategy to other strategies they have used in the past.
analysis or discussion of prior work	revisits a previous task with a new purpose	students can justify or explain the mathematics related to a familiar task.
opportunities to generalize patterns and big ideas	applies the same concept in another context	students can notice larger mathematical patterns and consider how the mathematics works in different situations.

You might be wondering if this analysis work is something you can do daily rather than weekly. You certainly can! The more you analyze data for whole-class trends, the more natural it will feel and the more efficient you will become. If you are just getting started, analyzing the data at the end of the week, just as Vicky did, is a nice way to ease into the habit. With time, you will likely begin to notice trends each day which you can use to tweak or alter the following day's math task.

Analyzing Data to Inform Individual or Small-Group Instruction

While conferring data cannot tell us which students have the same mathematical abilities, nor should it be used to level students, it can show us which students are grappling with the same big ideas and concepts at one particular moment in time. Providing additional learning opportunities for small groups of students should always be done in ways that support students with developing and maintaining positive beliefs about their mathematical abilities. For this reason, one important consideration to make is how to provide students with targeted support. At times there may be a need to engage a small group of students in a math task. Other times, this support can be embedded into classroom centers or games. Let's explore two types of mathematical needs you may notice in your conferring data and examples of how you might use that information to support your students (**Table 9.3**).

TABLE 9.3

Providing Support That Matches Students' Needs

Type of Support Needed	What This Support Could Look Like	Teacher's Role	How to Maintain and Support Positive Math Identities	1st Grade Example	5th Grade Example
Fluency	Embedded in centers, games, or practice opportunities	Teacher chooses particular centers or games for students based on the needs identified in the conferring data. Teacher confers with students as they work.	Students should experience other times when they are able to select their own centers or games. Students should observe that all students in the class have times when they need additional practice.	Giving students an opportunity to practice using known strategies to add within 10.	Giving students an opportunity to develop procedural fluency when multiplying multi-digit whole numbers using the standard algorithm.
Conceptual Understanding	Small group task	Teacher facilitates the task and discussion.	All small groups should be flexible and should not include the same students each time. Students should see that all students in the class participate in small groups to extend their learning.	Giving students an opportunity to represent two expressions with objects and explain how to determine if the two expressions are equal.	Giving students an opportunity to model and describe each step of the standard algorithm for multiplication of two-digit numbers.

Using the Data to Analyze Your Teaching

You might have noticed that the conferring notes document provides a space to indicate the types of conferences you have with your students. This is important information that you can use to analyze conferring trends over time. Let's look at a few different ways that you can use this data to reflect on your conferring practices.

Trends in Types of Conferences

There will be times when you do more conferring *Within the Task* and other times when you do more conferring *Beyond the Task*. These patterns could be related to the concept you are teaching, or it might be related to the timing of the unit. For example, you may notice you do more conferring *Within the Task* in the beginning of a unit. It is helpful to gather your conferring documents from the last few weeks and analyze them for those trends. Here are a few guiding questions that you can use:

- What type of conference have I been using most frequently?
- Why might I be using that type of conference the most? Is the choice to use that conference type related to what students need or is it related to my comfort with that type of conference?
- What, if any, changes might I make to my conferring patterns in the coming weeks?

Trends in Who Gets Which Type of Conference

Because conferring *Beyond the Task* engages students in developing conjectures, you want to make sure that all students are given this opportunity. Look at the types of conferences you have with each of your students. Here are a few guiding questions that you can use to reflect on your conferring patterns:

- Which students have I nudged to develop a conjecture?
- Are there any students that have not been nudged to develop a conjecture? What might be an opportunity to engage them in this work?
- Which students might be ready to make a broader generalization in the coming weeks?

Trends in Your Conferring Pace

Your conferring notes also tell the story of how frequently you are conferring and about how many students you meet with each week. Take a look at your conferring notes to notice these trends. You can use the following guiding questions to support this work:

- How many students do I confer with each week?
- How many weeks does it take me to meet with all of my students?
- What changes, if any, do I want to see in my conferring pace in the coming weeks? How will I achieve these goals?

Analyzing conferring data to make instructional decisions doesn't have to take a lot of time to make a big impact on student learning. Consider easing into the work and setting a manageable data analysis schedule for yourself. As you plan your week, think about when you might be able to spend about fifteen to twenty minutes analyzing your conferring data. As time goes on, you may decide to analyze the data more often, but give yourself the grace to ease into the process. Most importantly, remember that the purpose of analyzing conferring data is to learn more about your students' mathematical thinking, so that you can nudge them toward deeper understanding.

Cathy Fosnot, author of *Conferring with Young Mathematicians at Work*, acknowledges that sometimes educators are encouraged to use formative data in counterproductive ways. She states that "the current wave of 'data-driven' instruction promotes the use of formative assessment to determine 'who got the intended learning and who didn't' so that teachers can then teach even more directly to a list of prescribed outcomes, this time with smaller, more homogenous groups" (2016, 110). Using data as a way to level and label students will undoubtedly make analyzing conferring data a cumbersome and frustrating process. The data cannot yield this type of information, nor is this use of the data helpful for students' long-term learning or identities as capable mathematicians. Instead, my hope is that you will carve out some time each week to gather your notes and perhaps a few colleagues with only one goal on the agenda: learning something new about the mathematicians in your classroom!

Chapter 9 Planning for Data Collection and Analysis

Chapter 10

Planning for the Tricky Parts

Some of my favorite small moments in teaching are the ones that happen when I am conferring with mathematicians. I think of the times when students talk a mile a minute because they are so eager to share something new that they tried. I think of the times when I talk with students about their work and notice looks of pride and accomplishment on their faces that perhaps I hadn't seen before. I think about how I look forward to each day I get to confer with students because conferring is a time for us to gather and work as mathematicians. But, as with any teaching practice, there will be days when things don't go as planned. You will likely encounter hiccups on your conferring journey, and you may even encounter larger obstacles that perhaps leave you wondering if you should abandon conferring during math time altogether. But just as we ask our students to persevere and work through challenging situations, we too can find ways to navigate through these problems. After all, making time to talk with our mathematicians isn't a practice we want to let go of. Let's talk about a few obstacles to conferring that may arise and some strategies that may help you work through them.

The "Naming Strengths" Obstacle: *What if there isn't a clear strength to name and reinforce during the conference?*

All students have mathematical strengths. Yet, the problem of not being able to identify and articulate a strength within the time frame of a five-minute conference is a reality and a hiccup I encounter from time to time. The real problem isn't that there are no strengths to notice. Instead, the problem is either that we haven't uncovered enough of the students' thinking or that the students aren't far enough along in their work on the task. There are two productive approaches to this dilemma. First, you can continue to ask *probing thinking* questions. Questions such as, "Can you tell me more about your thinking?" or "Can you tell me more about why you made that decision?" might help you to elicit students' thinking so that you can identify strengths. Something that helps me in these moments is to embrace the silence. After asking a few *probing thinking* questions, I often just sit back and watch the students at work. Sometimes their mathematical thinking is revealed through conversation, but other times it is revealed by watching them as they engage in problem solving with their peers.

The second approach is appropriate for times when you need to move on to confer with another group or when perhaps you are conferring with a group of students that isn't far enough into their work for you to engage in a full conference. For times like these, you can name a strength that is related to the way students are tackling the task or collaborating with their peers. This might sound like, "I see that you are re-reading the task and asking each other questions about what the problem is about. Ensuring that everyone understands the task is an important first step for mathematicians when they collaborate to solve a problem." In these instances, you may decide not to engage in a full conference. Naming a strength, such as the one given in this example, may be sufficient at that moment in time. You might try conferring with another group and coming back to this group when they are further along.

The "I Work Alone" Obstacle: *Some students seem to prefer to work alone. Is it okay for students to work independently?*

There is no denying that collaboration and group work is beneficial for students. Yet, there is also value in having the time and space to think through mathematical ideas independently. One strategy for this obstacle is to provide students with a specified amount of time to work on problems independently before transitioning into group work. This strategy is helpful not only for students who prefer time to think through problems independently, but also because it may have the added benefit of increasing the variety and quality of ideas shared within the group. Oftentimes, when students join a group without think time, a few students may share the first idea that comes to mind. Without any other ideas on the table, one of these ideas may be accepted by the group without much thoughtful consideration. However, when all students have time to think through a problem on their own prior to meeting in a group, there are often a greater number of more robust ideas shared and more students doing the sharing.

Even with time to work independently, some students may still be reluctant to work with a group. These working patterns are important to notice. Students that choose to work on their own might make that decision for a variety of reasons. Consider taking notes about what patterns you notice as students work on their math tasks. Do they start off with a group and then begin working on their own? Do they seem to avoid working with a group altogether? When they are working in a group, do they appear comfortable sharing their ideas?

We should not expect that group work in math class will always go smoothly. Just like any other skill, working together must be explicitly practiced and reflected on to be productive. For example, you might try ending math time with an exit slip that asks students to note one thing that is going well with their math partner or group and one thing that is challenging. Later, you might spend some time brainstorming with students about how to work on a common challenge of working with a partner or with a group. You might even guide your students to set goals for how group work can be strengthened. Teaching students to work productively in a group is time well spent that will benefit them not only when engaged in mathematics, but across and beyond the school day.

Even with practice and support, requiring students to work together may not lead to a true collaborative experience. To be meaningful to students, working alongside their peers should feel purposeful. Consider looking for students who are using a related strategy or working on similar conjectures and asking them if they'd like to work together. Inviting students to work together for a common purpose suggests to them that their ideas are important and that the purpose of working together is to share and enhance those ideas. Working together shouldn't be something students feel they have to do, but rather something that mathematicians do when they want to share ideas and work toward a common goal.

The "I'm Done" Obstacle: Some students are finished working on a task before the teacher is finished conferring with other students. What should early finishers do when they are done working on a task?

We all have those moments when we wish we could clone ourselves because there simply is no way to support every student at once. If you are feeling this way when you are conferring, it may be because students are approaching you while you are conferring to either ask for help or tell you that they are finished with their work. You may be thinking to yourself that if you could just get over to that group, you could nudge them *Beyond the Task* and get them working on a conjecture. You might also be thinking that you could help a group that feels stuck by getting them to talk through their thinking. These feelings of wanting to support everyone at once are completely normal. There are a couple of strategies that might help.

The first strategy is to continue to develop a classroom culture in which students feel capable and empowered to make decisions about how they will conduct their mathematical work for the day. Consider making an anchor chart (**Figure 10.1**) that gives students ideas about the different ways they can spend their time. For some classrooms it may work best to add ideas to this chart throughout the year. For other classrooms, especially in the primary grades, it may work best to have a chart that is specific to the unit students are working on. Revisit the chart periodically as a class and use it to check in with students about how they spend their time.

FIGURE 10.1
Anchor charts from fifth-grade (*top*) and kindergarten (*bottom*) classrooms provide ideas for what students can work on when they are finished with a math task

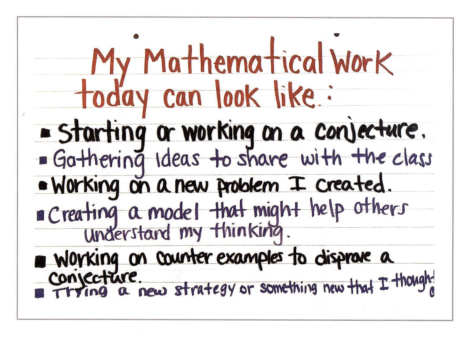

Part 4   Planning for Success: What Should You Consider Before Conferring?

Sometimes teachers might give students a different assignment to complete when they are finished with a math task. While there are times when this might make sense for students, it isn't necessary or even feasible to always have extra assignments at the ready for early finishers. Instead, we can focus on giving students the tools and encouragement they need to go deeper within and beyond the task that they are working on.

The second strategy is to conduct a mid-class share out. This strategy is especially useful when you notice that some students appear to be "stuck" with the task. As you confer with students and notice interesting ideas and strategies, consider stopping the class for a quick share out. This quick share does not need to be a formal community share in which students gather together and a group of students shares their work under a document camera or on the board. Instead, this can be an informal verbal share out to highlight the work that one group is doing in the hopes that it sparks ideas for other groups. This might sound like, "Let's take a quick pause. Daniel and Jun just tried something pretty neat. Let's give them a few minutes to explain what they tried." After the students share, you might add something as brief as, "Maybe you'll decide to try Daniel and Jun's idea out today or another day."

You might also follow up with a reminder that when they feel stuck, they should visit other groups to see what they are doing. As mathematicians, we share ideas with one another, and those ideas make us stronger. The mid-class share out and frequent reminders to get ideas from their peers helps develop a classroom math community in which students are at the center, rather than the teacher.

The "Time" Obstacle: *Some days there isn't enough time for students to work on a task and develop a conjecture. Can this work extend over more than one day?*

Absolutely! Writing and revising conjectures takes time. Students can continue this work across multiple days. But what about the math tasks on those subsequent days? Won't they miss opportunities to work on those tasks? Possibly. As you plan the week, think about the tasks that you are giving students. If a group would like to work on their conjecture on the following day, consider the content and context of that task. If the tasks are similar and give students exposure to the same concept in a very similar context, then perhaps giving them the opportunity to delve into their conjecture rather than the task would be just as beneficial. If the task is not one that you'd be okay with them missing out on, consider having them explore the task and then work on the conjecture. You might also have times when you ask students to pause on the conjecture so that they can participate in today's math task and then resume the following day. The key is to think about what learning experiences are going to be most beneficial for students.

The "Revisiting Conjectures" Obstacle: *Students' conjectures are displayed on the classroom walls, but students are not revisiting them.*

The purpose of displaying students' conjectures in the classroom is for the conjectures to become living documents that are referred to and revised throughout the year. One way to encourage students to revisit the conjectures is by taking time every couple of weeks for a *Conjecture Tour*. This tour could be done by having students visit the displayed conjectures in small groups, read them together, and ask themselves if they think that any of them can be disproven or need to be revised. As students deepen their mathematical understanding and their abilities to communicate with precision, they may decide that some conjectures can be disproven and might want an opportunity to gather evidence or counterexamples. Or they may decide that the words used in some of the conjectures need to be revised using more precise mathematical vocabulary. Taking *Conjecture Tours* regularly keeps students thinking critically about the conjectures and the mathematics. It also reminds students that their work is important and worthy of being revisited throughout the year.

The decision to start a new teaching practice is a big one. Time is limited, and because of that, we know each moment with students must be intentional. One of the great things about conferring is that it doesn't require additional instructional time; instead, it is a different way to use the time we have with students. As you embark on your conferring journey, know that there will be easy days and there will be hard days, but *every day* will be a day that you talked with students and got to know them a little more. By conferring you aren't just teaching mathematics, you are creating a mathematics community in which students are engaging daily as mathematicians.

For some students, engaging in mathematics in ways in which they are treated as strong, capable mathematicians who are entrusted to make important mathematical decisions will be a new experience and a new way of learning math. Dr. Jo Boaler, professor of mathematics education at Stanford University, shared that after conducting several research studies it became evident to her that many students do not see mathematics for what it really is. She stated, "Ask most school students what math is and they will tell you it is a list of rules and procedures that need to be remembered" (2008, 19). The way students view mathematics, including the purpose of mathematics and their place in mathematics, has everything to do with the experiences they have in school. As Dr. Boaler suggests, "Bringing mathematics back to life for schoolchildren involves giving them a sense of living mathematics. When students are given an opportunity to ask their own questions and to extend problems into new directions, they know mathematics is still alive, not something that has already been decided and just needs to be memorized" (2008, 27). As you think about conferring and how you might implement this practice into your classroom, consider reflecting on the experiences you want your students to remember when they think of learning math and specifically when they think of learning math in your classroom. How do you want them to see themselves in the world of mathematics? What do you want your students to say at the end of the year when you ask them, "What is math?"

Appendix A

If/Then Charts

Early Numeracy Skills to Name and Reinforce If/Then

If the student is . . .	Then you might say . . .
touching each object as they count	I noticed that you touched each object as you were counting. Why did you do that?
pushing objects together in groups as they count	What a great way to keep track while you are counting.
counting a set of objects more than once	I noticed that you counted that set and then counted it again. Why did you do that? I think you are right. Counting again is important to do when the first count doesn't seem right.
suggesting that a fellow mathematician count again or that a count is incorrect	I noticed you suggested that your group should count again. Sharing ideas and giving helpful suggestions is an important part of being a member of a math community.
subitizing and counting on	I noticed that you only touched some counters. You started counting on at _____. Can you tell me more about how you did that? You figured out that counting on can be much more efficient than counting each object one by one.
organizing objects in lines or groups	What an interesting way to organize the objects. Why did you group them like that? The way you organized the counters seems helpful for counting them and noticing which groups have more or less.
estimating	I heard you say that you had more/fewer/the same amount of counters as your last collection even before you started to count. How did you know that? You estimated the number of counters you had and made a reasonable guess. This is a helpful thing to do before counting a collection of objects, so you can know if the amount you count makes sense.
adjusting an estimate	I noticed that you changed your estimate. Why did you do that? Knowing that you can change an estimate when you have new ideas or information is really important.
recording their ideas	What did you write down? What a great way to keep track of your thinking and to share your ideas with others.

Appendix A   Conferring in the Math Classroom   **125**

If/Then Charts (continued)

Early Numeracy Skills to Name and Reinforce If/Then

If the student is...	Then you might say...
counting more than one object at a time	As I was listening, I heard you counting but not by ones. Can you tell me more about your counting? You used counting patterns to skip count. That is an efficient way to count a collection of objects.
using what is known about one quantity to describe another quantity	How did you know that this collection was more/less than _____? Describing and comparing collections of objects seems like a good way to think about how many you have. Mathematicians can use what they know about one collection to describe another collection.
using knowledge of number parts to count, add, or subtract	I notice that you added/subtracted/counted _____. Where did that number come from? What a useful idea. Breaking numbers into smaller parts can be helpful when you are counting/adding/subtracting.
drawing pictures of objects to count, add, or subtract	What did you draw here? Your drawing really helps explain what is going on in this problem.
drawing dots or symbols to represent objects to count, add, or subtract	I see you made dots. What are those? What a helpful strategy. Drawing dots instead of _____ is a really efficient way to record what is happening.

Grades 2–5 Skills to Name and Reinforce If/Then

If the student is...	Then you might say...
using the associative property of addition $a + b + c = (a + b) + c = a + (b + c)$	You mentioned that you grouped these addends together and added them instead of adding the numbers in the order they were listed in the problem. Why did you choose to group the numbers in that way? Using the associative property of addition can help you group and add numbers in ways that make sense to you. This shows your flexibility as a mathematician.
using the associative property of multiplication $a \times b \times c = (a \times b) \times c = a \times (b \times c)$	You mentioned that you grouped these two factors together and multiplied them instead of multiplying the numbers in the order they were listed in the problem. Why did you choose to group the numbers in that way? Using the associative property of multiplication can help you group and multiply numbers in ways that make sense to you. This shows your flexibility as a mathematician.

If/Then Charts (continued)

Grades 2–5 Skills to Name
Reinforce If/Then (continued)

If the student is...	Then you might say...
using the commutative property of addition a + b = b + a	So, are you saying that you thought of this problem as 8 + 2 rather than 2 + 8 because you felt it was easier to think about? Your decision to use the commutative property of addition enabled you to problem solve in a way that made sense to you and was efficient given those numbers. As a mathematician you know how useful it is to think flexibly.
using the commutative property of multiplication a × b = b × a	So, are you saying that you thought of this problem as 0.5 × 50 rather than 50 × 0.5 because you felt it was easier to think about? Your decision to use the commutative property of multiplication enabled you to problem solve in a way that made sense to you and was efficient given those numbers. As a mathematician you know how useful it is to think flexibly.
using a number sense strategy to add/subtract/multiply/divide	So, you're saying that you [name strategy the student used]. That strategy seemed to help you add/subtract/multiply/divide.
rethinking their work because something doesn't make sense or isn't reasonable	You mentioned that you are going to start over/rethink your work because your answer isn't reasonable. This is an important mathematical skill. It is important to stop and think again when something doesn't seem right.
drawing a visual representation/creating a model	Your decision to draw a visual representation/make a model seemed to help you understand the problem. Visuals are an important tool for mathematicians because they help you to understand and communicate ideas.
estimating	So, you estimated first? Estimating is an important skill for mathematicians. It really helps you to know if you are on the right track or if you need to rethink your strategy.
using a second strategy to check their work	So, you are doing it this way just to be sure you get the same results? Using a second strategy is a great way to make sure that your answer is correct. The ability to move flexibly between strategies is a helpful way to check your work so you can communicate correct and precise information.
analyzing a data representation	So, it seems like you analyzed the graph/chart/information before you made any strategy decisions. Taking the time to notice how the data are represented and organized before making quick decisions can help you interpret data representations with accuracy.
connecting previous math knowledge to new mathematical learning	So, you said that you knew _____ and wondered if it would work for _____. You understand how useful is it to actively look for connections between what you are working on and what you already know.

Appendix A   Conferring in the Math Classroom   **127**

Appendix B

Conferring Scenario Cards

K–1 Card A

 What would you name? What would you reinforce?

Two students are playing a dice game with an addition and subtraction spinner. One student has 15 counters in front of them. The student rolls a 6 and the spinner lands on the subtraction symbol. The student removes two from their counters and then counts 3, 4, 5, 6 to remove a total of six.

K–1 Card B

 What would you name? What would you reinforce?

One student has grouped their counters into piles of 10. To uncover the student's thinking, you ask what they are working on. They reply, "I am trying to make 100. So far I have 1, 2, 3, 4, 5, 6, 7, 8, 9, 10, 11, 12, 13, 14, 15, 16, 17, 18, 19, 20."

K–1 Card C

 What would you name? What would you reinforce?

A student is making sets of counters using a number spinner. The student spins and lands on the number 9. The students begins to take counters out of the bag. As the student grabs them, they count "1, 2, 3, 4, 5, 6, 7, 8, 9, 10, 11. Oops." Then the students puts all the counters back and starts over.

K–1 Card D

 What would you name? What would you reinforce?

A student is making sets of counters using a number spinner. The student spins and it lands on the number 4. The student already has a collection of five counters in front of them. The student looks down and touches each of the original five counters and says, "1, 2, 3, 4." Then they push the remaining counter to the side.

K–1 Card E

**What would you name?
What would you reinforce?**

Two students are sorting small dinosaur counters by color. One student says, "Look! I have more red ones than you."

K–1 Card F

**What would you name?
What would you reinforce?**

Two students are working together with connecting cubes. You ask, "What are you working on?" One student replies, "We are making trains. Look how long mine is!" The other student says, "Yeah, but mine has more than yours."

K–1 Card G

**What would you name?
What would you reinforce?**

A student has placed 33 counters into three piles of 10 and three ones. The students counts objects, "10, 20, 30, 31, 32, 33. Wait. 10, 20, 30, 31, 32, 33. Yeah. 33."

2–3 Card A

**What would you name?
What would you reinforce?**

Two students are working with fraction circles. One student says, "Is this the $\frac{1}{8}$ piece?" The other student replies, "No, that's way too big. One-eighth is a small piece."

2–3 Card B

What would you name? What would you reinforce?

Students were asked to draw pictures with equal groups and create a story to go with the picture that represents division. You notice that one student drew six bags with five pieces of candy in each bag. Their partner says, "This is 6 times 5. Wait, the candy is divided into 5 groups. I don't know."

2–3 Card C

What would you name? What would you reinforce?

Two students are working together to determine how a group of polygons have been sorted. As they look at the shapes, one student says, "I think they are sorted by the number of sides." The other student says, "I think so too, but I also think they are sorted by the number of corners. Look, they have the same number of corners."

2–3 Card D

What would you name? What would you reinforce?

Groups of students were asked to count cups full of counters. As you approach one group, you hear a student say they need to dump out the cups and start counting. You hear another student say, "Let's make an array." A third student says, "Maybe we can make more than one array since there are so many counters."

2–3 Card E

What would you name? What would you reinforce?

Students were asked to work in pairs and record their thoughts about several images. Each image is an array that represents an eights multiplication fact. One group labels all the arrays with multiplication equations. One student says, "I think the answer to an eights fact will always be even."

Appendix B   Conferring in the Math Classroom

2–3 Card F

What would you name? What would you reinforce?

Three students are playing a fraction game. The first student spins the spinner and it lands on ¼. Another student says, "One-fourth. We need to find the shape with four parts." Another student says, "Look. We already colored in three parts. That was the last fraction we needed for that shape. Now we can color in the last part."

2–3 Card G

What would you name? What would you reinforce?

Two students are playing a sorting game in which one partner sorts the shape and the other guesses how they sorted. After one student sorts the shapes, the other student says, "I think you put all the quadrilaterals together. Wait, no, maybe not. This one here has more than four sides. I need to think some more."

4–5 Card A

What would you name? What would you reinforce?

Two students are working together to add two fractions. One student says, " 9/8 and 10/8 are both bigger than 1." So, our answer isn't right.

4–5 Card B

What would you name? What would you reinforce?

Two students are comparing the numbers 36.68 and 35.678. One student says, "I put a zero after 35.68 because it is easier for me to compare them."

132 Appendix B   Conferring in the Math Classroom

4–5 Card C

What would you name? What would you reinforce?

Students are ordering a set of four fractions from least to greatest. One student says, "$4/8$ is the same as $1/2$ because 4 is half of 8."

4–5 Card D

What would you name? What would you reinforce?

A group of students decide that they need to divide 5 by $1/2$. One student draws a visual representation of five wholes and then says he isn't sure what to do next.

4–5 Card E

What would you name? What would you reinforce?

Two students decide to add $5/6$ and $1/2$. One student says, "We need to find a common denominator." The other student says, "I think we can break them apart. Let's change $5/6$ to $1/2$ and $2/6$. Then let's add the halves together to get 1 whole and $2/6$."

4–5 Card F

What would you name? What would you reinforce?

Three students are analyzing a dot plot. One student shares his ideas. Another student says, "That doesn't seem right. Oh, wait. It is because we didn't look at the key. One dot equals 100 miles, not 1 mile."

Appendix B   Conferring in the Math Classroom   133

4–5 Card G

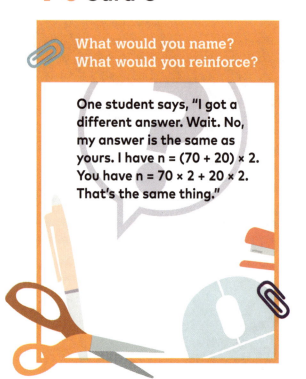

What would you name? What would you reinforce?

One student says, "I got a different answer. Wait. No, my answer is the same as yours. I have n = (70 + 20) × 2. You have n = 70 × 2 + 20 × 2. That's the same thing."

Appendix C

Conferring Notes Template

Math Conferring Data (*Week of*) _____

Unit: _____

Named and Reinforced:	**Named and Reinforced:**	**Named and Reinforced:**	**Named and Reinforced:**
Nudged to:	**Nudged to:**	**Nudged to:**	**Nudged to:**
Within Task **Beyond Task**	**Within Task** **Beyond Task**	**Within Task** **Beyond Task**	**Within Task** **Beyond Task**

Appendix C Conferring in the Math Classroom

References

Anderson, Carl. 2000. *How's It Going? A Practical Guide to Conferring with Student Writers.* Portsmouth, NH: Heinemann.

Boaler, Jo. 2008. *What's Math Got to Do With It?* New York, NY: Penguin Books.

Beilock, Sian L., Elizabeth A. Gunderson, Gerardo Ramirez, and Susan C. Levine. 2010. "Female Teachers' Math Anxiety Affects Girls' Math Achievement." *Proceedings of the National Academy of Sciences of the United States of America* 107, no. 5: 1860–1863. https://doi.org/10.1073/pnas.0910967107.

Calkins, Lucy. 1994. *The Art of Teaching Writing.* Portsmouth, NH: Heinemann.

Calkins, Lucy, Amanda Hartman, and Zoe White. 2005. *One to One: The Art of Conferring with Young Writers.* Portsmouth, NH: Heinemann.

Fosnot, Catherine. 2016. *Conferring with Young Mathematicians at Work: Making Moments Matter.* New London, CT: New Perspectives on Learning.

National Council of Teachers of Mathematics (NCTM). 2014. *Principles to Action: Ensuring Mathematics Success for All.* Reston, VA: NCTM.

Ramirez, Gerardo, Sophia Yang Hooper, Nicole B. Kersting, Ronald Ferguson, and David Yeager. 2018. "Teacher Math Anxiety Relates to Adolescent Students' Math Achievement." *Aera Open* 4, no. 1: 1–13. https://doi.org/10.1177/2332858418756052.

Small, Marian. 2019. *Understanding the Math We Teach and How to Teach It.* Portsmouth, NH: Stenhouse.

Zager, Tracy Johnston. 2017. *Becoming the Math Teacher You Wish You'd Had: Ideas and Strategies from Vibrant Classrooms.* Portland, ME: Stenhouse.

Index

A

addition, 71t, 72t, 84t, 125–127
analyzing data representations, 73t, 126–127
anchor charts, 18–19, 88, 89f
Anderson, Carl, 83
Art of Teaching Writing, The (Calkins), 17
assessment, 8t, 9–10
asset-based conferring. *See* strengths-based conferring
associative property, 72t, 84t, 126–127

B

Bearden, Loretta, 99, 100–103
Becoming the Math Teacher You Wish You'd Had (Zager), 21
Beyond the Task conference structure. *See also* types of math conferences
    compared to *Within the Task* conference structure, 33
    data gathering and analysis, 107f–108f, 113
    decisions regarding, 32, 33, 35–36, 56f–57f, 113
    example of, 85–86
    with kindergarten students, 91–92
    nudge thinking beyond the task component of conferences and, 83
    overview, 27, 30–33, 34t
    predictability in conferences and, 83
    questioning and, 51t, 53–59
Boaler, Dr. Jo, 123

C

Calkins, Lucy, 17
Chrischna, Katie, 49–59
classroom culture, 119–121. *See also* math community
collaborative work. *See also* group work
    comparing math and writing conferences and, 17t
    example of, 86–90
    math community and, 100–103
    naming and reinforcing, 4, 69t
    obstacles to conferring and, 118–119, 121
community, math. *See* math community
community share, 93–95, 121. *See also* math community; sharing ideas
commutative property, 72t, 84t, 126–127
conceptual understanding, 112f
conferring beyond the task. *See Beyond the Task* conference structure
conferring data. *See* data from math conferences
conferring from strengths. *See* strengths-based conferring
conferring notes template
    complete, 137
    data analysis and, 110, 113–114
    examples of, 107f–108f
    overview, 107
conferring scenario cards, 73, 74f, 129–134

conferring within the task. *See Within the Task* conference structure
Conferring with Young Mathematicians at Work (Fosnot), 114
conjecture, mathematical. *See also* invite conjecture and sharing component of conferences; nudge thinking beyond the task component of conferences
    Beyond the Task conference structure, 34t
    example of, 85–90
    with kindergarten students, 91–92
    obstacles to conferring and, 119–121, 122
    overview, 32–33, 84–85
    predictability in conferences and, 83
    question types and, 51t
    revisiting conjectures, 122
    sharing during community share, 93–95
    types of math conferences and, 35t
    using data to identify trends and analyze teaching, 113
Conjecture Tours, 122
connections between concepts and ideas. *See also* listening to student thinking
    Beyond the Task conference structure, 30, 34t
    If-Then charts and, 73t, 126–127
    Within the Task conference structure, 29t
    types of math conferences and, 35t
conversations, math, 5–11, 74–79. *See also* listening to student thinking
counting
    conjectures and, 84t, 91–92
    conversations and, 9–11
    If-Then charts and, 70t–71t, 125–126
creativity
    comparing math and writing conferences and, 18–21
    goals of math conferences and, 82
    naming and reinforcing, 69t

D

Dante, Elysha, 90–92
data from math conferences
    analyzing to identify trends and inform instruction, 109–114
    gathering, 106–107, 108f
    overview, 106
decimals, 84t
decision making
    Beyond the Task conference structure, 32, 33, 34t, 35–36, 56f–57f, 113
    comparing math and writing conferences and, 18–21
    funneling pattern of questioning and, 44t
    Within the Task conference structure, 29t, 32, 33, 35–36, 54–55, 56f–57f, 113
    types of math conferences and, 35t
decision making, mathematical. *See* naming mathematical decisions
deep conversations, 5–11, 74–79. *See also* strengths-based conferring

deep listening. *See* listening to student thinking
dependent learning, 44t. *See also* learning
directed paraphrasing formative assessment, 74–79, 75f
direct modeling, 17t, 18–21
discovery. *See also* conjecture, mathematical
    comparing math and writing conferences and, 18–21
    questioning that funnel students' thinking and ideas, 44–46
    types of math conferences and, 35t
disposition, 69t
distributive property, 85–90, 93–95
division, 72t, 126–127
drafts, 86–90

E

early finishers, 119–121
early numeracy skills, 70t–71t, 125–126
Encouraging Reflection and Justification question type, 50, 51t
engagement
    goals of math conferences and, 26–27
    overview, 123
    types of math conferences and, 35t, 36
errors, noticing and responding to, 66–68
estimating, 70t, 72t, 125–127
exploration. *See also* conjecture, mathematical
    comparing math and writing conferences and, 18–21
    goals of math conferences and, 82
    questioning that funnel students' thinking and ideas, 44–46
    types of math conferences and, 35t

F

feedback, 18
finishing work early, 119–121
fluency, 112f
formative assessment, 74–79, 114
Fosnot, Cathy, 114
fractions, 84t
funneling pattern of questioning, 44–46, 47. *See also* questioning

G

Gathering Information question type, 50, 51t
generalizations. *See also* connections between concepts and ideas
    Beyond the Task conference structure, 34t
    If-Then charts and, 70t, 73t, 125–127
    naming and reinforcing, 69t
    questioning and, 55
    types of math conferences and, 35t
geometry, 84t
grades 2–5 skills, 72t–73t, 126–127
grouping of students
    analyzing data to identify trends and inform instruction, 112
    math community and, 102, 103
    overview, 105
grouping tasks, 70t, 125–126
group work, 112, 118–119. *See also* collaborative work

H

hypotheses, mathematical. *See* conjecture, mathematical

I

identity, math. *See* math identity
If-Then charts
    early numeracy skills, 70t–71t, 125–126
    grades 2–5 skills, 72t–73t, 126–127
    strengths-based conferring and, 69, 70t–73t
independent learning, 44t, 118–119. *See also* learning
instruction, data analysis and, 109–114
invite conjecture and sharing component of conferences. *See also* conjecture, mathematical; invite sharing component of conferences; sharing ideas
    Beyond the Task conference structure, 30, 34t
    overview, 84–85
    questioning and, 51t, 57f
invite sharing component of conferences. *See also* invite conjecture and sharing component of conferences; sharing ideas
    questioning and, 51t, 54t, 57f, 58t
    Within the Task conference structure, 28, 29t

K

Kellog, Jessica, 9–10

L

level-based grouping of students. *See* grouping of students
literacy conferences, 13–15, 16–21

M

Making the Mathematics Visible question type, 50, 51t
math community. *See also* sharing ideas
    Beyond the Task conference structure, 34t
    building, 100–103
    community share, 93–95, 121
    conjecture and, 32–33, 93–95
    obstacles to conferring and, 119–121
math conferences. *See also* community share; strengths-based conferring; types of math conferences
    compared to writing conferences, 16–21
    goals of, 23–27
    obstacles to conferring and, 117–123
    overview, 4–7, 123
    types of math conversations and, 7–11
math conversations, 5–11, 74–79. *See also* listening to student thinking
mathematical conjectures. *See* conjecture, mathematical
mathematical understanding. *See* understanding, mathematical
math identity
    math community and, 100–103
    overview, xii–xiii
    reinforcing, 18
    strengths-based conferring and, 79
    teacher math identity, xiii
measuring tasks, 10–11, 84t, 109–114
mentor text, comparing math and writing conferences and, 17t

mixed ability groups. *See* grouping of students
model creation, 72*t*, 126–127
modeling, comparing math and writing conferences and, 17*t*, 18–21
multiplication, 72*t*, 85–90, 93–95, 126–127

N

name and reinforce component of conferences. *See also* naming mathematical decisions; naming students' strengths; reinforcement
    Beyond the Task conference structure, 30, 34*t*
    conferring scenario cards and, 73, 74*f*, 129–134
    If-Then charts and, 69, 70*t*–73*t*, 125–127
    questioning and, 51*t*, 54*t*, 56*f*, 58*t*, 82–83
    strengths-based conferring and, 68–69, 69*t*, 70*t*–73*t*
    Within the Task conference structure, 28, 29*t*
naming mathematical decisions. *See also* name and reinforce component of conferences; naming students' strengths
    Beyond the Task conference structure, 34*t*
    If-Then charts and, 69, 70*t*–73*t*, 125–127
    question types and, 51*t*
naming students' strengths. *See also* name and reinforce component of conferences; naming mathematical decisions; strengths-based conferring
    Beyond the Task conference structure, 30
    comparing math and writing conferences and, 17
    conferring notes template, 107*f*–108*f*, 137
    gathering data and, 107, 108*f*
    If-Then charts and, 69, 70*t*–73*t*, 125–127
    math identity and, 79
    obstacles to conferring and, 118
    overview, 4
    practicing and preparing for, 73–79
    strengths-based conferring and, 79
    Within the Task conference structure, 28
National Council of Teachers of Mathematics (NCTM), 50, 55, 58*t*
notice and understand component of conferences. *See also* observing in math conferences
    Beyond the Task conference structure, 30, 34*t*
    example of, 51–53
    If-Then charts and, 69, 70*t*–73*t*
    questioning and, 51*t*, 54*t*, 56*f*, 58*t*
    Within the Task conference structure, 28, 29*t*
nudge thinking beyond the task component of conferences. *See also Beyond the Task* conference structure
    conferring notes template, 107*f*–108*f*, 137
    example of, 85–90
    with kindergarten students, 91–92
    overview, 30, 34*t*
    questioning and, 51*t*, 57*f*, 82–83
number sense, 72*t*, 84*t*, 126–127

O

observing in math conferences. *See also* notice and understand component of conferences
    Beyond the Task conference structure, 30, 34*t*
    comparing math and writing conferences and, 16, 17*t*
    goals of, 23–27
    overview, 4
    strengths-based conferring and, 65
    Within the Task conference structure, 28, 29*t*
    types of math conversations and, 7–11
One to One (Calkins, Hartman, & White), 68–69, 83
open tasks, 102, 103
organization tasks, 69*t*, 70*t*, 125–126
overdirecting student thinking, 44–46

P

patterns, 27, 28, 82
Paul, Jared, 10–11
placement. *See* data from math conferences; grouping of students
pocket chart, 88, 89*f*
predictability, 83, 103
Principles to Actions (NCTM), 50
probing thinking questions, 50, 51*t*, 118. *See also* questioning
problem solving
    comparing math and writing conferences and, 17*t*, 18–21
    funneling pattern of questioning and, 44*t*
    obstacles to conferring and, 118
procedures, step-by-step. *See* step-by-step procedures

Q

questioning
    Beyond the Task conference structure, 34*t*
    funneling students' thinking and ideas with, 44–46
    improving, 47, 59
    nudge thinking beyond the task component of conferences and, 82–83
    obstacles to conferring and, 118
    overview, 41, 42–43, 50, 51–53, 51*t*
    purpose for, 47
    Within the Task conference structure, 29*t*
    types of math conferences and, 53–59
Questioning Support Document for Math Conferences, 50, 51*t*

R

recording ideas, 70*t*, 125–126
reflection. *See* Encouraging Reflection and Justification question type
reinforcement. *See also* name and reinforce component of conferences
    Beyond the Task conference structure, 30, 34*t*
    comparing math and writing conferences and, 18
    conferring notes template, 107*f*–108*f*, 137
    conferring scenario cards and, 73, 74*f*, 129–134
    gathering data and, 107, 108*f*
    If-Then charts and, 69, 70*t*–73*t*, 125–127
    obstacles to conferring and, 118
    questioning and, 51*t*, 83*t*
    Within the Task conference structure, 28
representations, 69*t*
responsiveness, funneling pattern of questioning and, 44*t*
revision, 86–90
revisiting conjectures, 122. *See also* conjecture, mathematical
Ruiz, Dana, 24–36

S

scaffolding learning, 8t, 10–11
share outs, 121
sharing ideas. *See also* invite conjecture and sharing component of conferences; invite sharing component of conferences; math community
    Beyond the Task conference structure, 34t
    community share, 93–95, 121
    conjecture and, 90, 91–92, 93–95
    example of, 5–7
    math community and, 102
    obstacles to conferring and, 121
    overview, 4–5
    questioning that funnel students' thinking and ideas, 44–46
    Within the Task conference structure, 28, 29t
Small, Marian, 84
small-group instruction, 112
step-by-step procedures, 18–21. *See also* strategy use and instruction
Stevens, Mitchell, 64–68, 74–79
strategy use and instruction. *See also* step-by-step procedures
    comparing math and writing conferences and, 17t, 18–21
    If-Then charts and, 69, 70t–73t, 126–127
    questioning that funnel students' thinking and ideas, 44–47
    question types and, 51t
    types of math conferences and, 35t
strengths-based conferring. *See also* math conferences; naming students' strengths
    conferring notes template, 107f–108f, 137
    example of, 64–65
    gathering data and, 107, 108f
    math identity and, 79
    noticing and responding to errors and, 66–68
    obstacles to conferring and, 118
    overview, 63–64
    practicing and preparing for, 73–79
    strengths to notice, name, and reinforce, 69t
structuring math blocks, 103, 119–121
struggle, 44t
student thinking outside of the classroom, 46. *See also* generalizations; listening to student thinking
subitizing, 70t, 125–126
subtraction, 71t, 72t, 125–127
symmetry, 100–103

T

task creation, data from math conferences and, 109–114
teacher math identity, xiii. *See also* math identity
teaching, using data to identify trends and analyze, 113–114
thinking, student. *See* listening to student thinking
Tijerina, Deb, 13–15, 16–21
time issues, 121
types of math conferences. *See also Beyond the Task* conference structure; math conferences; *Within the Task* conference structure
    decisions regarding, 32, 33, 35–36, 54–55, 56f–57f
    overview, 27
    questioning and, 51t, 53–59
    using data to identify trends and analyze teaching, 113

U

Uhler, Mark, 85–86, 93–95
uncover student thinking component of conferences. *See also* listening to student thinking
    Beyond the Task conference structure, 30, 34t
    questioning and, 51t, 54t, 56f, 58t
    Within the Task conference structure, 28, 29t
understanding, mathematical. *See also* learning
    analyzing data to identify trends and inform instruction, 112f
    goals of math conferences and, 26–27
    questioning and, 44–46, 44t
    Within the Task conference structure, 29t
    types of math conferences and, 35t
Understanding the Math We Teach and How to Teach It (Small), 84

V

visual representations, 51t, 71t, 72t, 125–127. *See also* conjecture, mathematical

W

Within the Task conference structure. *See also* types of math conferences
    compared to *Beyond the Task* conference structure, 33
    decisions regarding, 32, 33, 35–36, 54–55, 56f–57f, 113
    gathering data and, 107f–108f
    nudge thinking beyond the task component of conferences and, 83
    overview, 27, 28–30
    predictability in conferences and, 83
    questioning and, 51t, 53–59
    using data to identify trends and analyze teaching, 113
word wall, 88, 89f
work samples, 74–79
writing conferences, 13–15, 16–21

Z

Zager, Tracy, 21